TRUE CRIME :
VIRGINIA

The State's Most Notorious Criminal Cases

John F. Jebb

STACKPOLE BOOKS

Copyright ©2011 by Stackpole Books

Published by
STACKPOLE BOOKS
5067 Ritter Road
Mechanicsburg, PA 17055
www.stackpolebooks.com

Printed in the United States of America

10 9 8 7 6 5 4 3 2 1

FIRST EDITION

Cover design by Tessa J. Sweigert

Cover photos: Blood sample, ©Rob Byron/Shutterstock. The following photographs used with permission of the *Richmond Times-Dispatch*, clockwise: Governor L. Douglas Wilder on a surprise visit to the Richmond jail, June 6, 1990, photo by Bob Brown; Hokie Stone Memorial, after the shootings at Virginia Tech, April 19, 2007, photo by Eva Russo; Earl Washington Jr. after prison release with advocate Marie Deans, February 13, 2001, photo by Alexa Welch Edlund; Timothy Spencer surrounded by guards after trial, May 13, 1989, photo by Wallace Huey Clark; Jens Soering in prison, July 8, 2003, photo by Carlos Santos. The author thanks Andrea Bedson, Newsroom Office Manager at the *Times-Dispatch*, for arranging the use of these photos.

Library of Congress Cataloging-in-Publication Data

Jebb, John F.
  True crime : Virginia : the state's most notorious criminal cases / John F. Jebb. — 1st ed.
      p. cm.
  Includes bibliographical references.
  ISBN-13: 978-0-8117-0649-0 (pbk.)
  ISBN-10: 0-8117-0649-4 (pbk.)
  1. Violent crimes—Virginia—History—Case studies. I. Title.
  HV6793.V8J43 2011
  364.109755—dc22
                                              2011008545

Contents

Introduction

Virginians assert that their Commonwealth has a preeminent status in American history. They can point to impressive evidence. In 1619, the Virginia settlers elected the first representative assembly in the American colonies. In 1774, when the royal governor dissolved the restive assembly, its members convened in a tavern and called for a convention of representatives from the colonies to plot their future. Thus the movement to bring the colonies into a cooperative entity began in Virginia. In 1776, at the Continental Congress, John Adams insisted that Thomas Jefferson write the Declaration of Independence, saying, "You are a Virginian, and a Virginian ought to appear at the head of this business." (Adams gives this account in an 1822 letter.) Virginia provided four of the first five American presidents; Virginians held the office for thirty-two of the USA's first thirty-six years.

Virginia was an essential part of the South. Historians William J. Cooper Jr. and Thomas E. Terrill write of the South's pre–Civil War colleges, "Without question the University of Virginia was the most influential. Jefferson, its founder, was both the political and intellectual father of the university. . . Jefferson's university had the first elective curriculum in the country and introduced the teaching of modern foreign languages." Historian Avery O. Craven writes that in 1861, the seceding states actively wanted Virginia with them: "A new nation without Virginia would lack a genuine Southern quality. A movement without her approval and support could never be quite satisfactory. She was, after all, the founder and keeper of 'the Southern tradition.'" The Confederacy took Richmond, Virginia, as its capital city. In 1958, in a speech at the University of Virginia, Nobel Prize–winning author William Faulkner, from Mississippi, asked the Commonwealth to be a model of peaceful race relations: "And the place for this to begin is Virginia, the mother of all the rest of us of the South. . . So let it begin in Virginia, toward whom the rest of us are already looking as the child looks toward the parent for a sign, a signal where to go and how to go. . . I believe we will follow you." (Virginia did not become a leader in civil rights, and the speech endangered Faulkner's status at UVA as a writer in residence.) In 1989, L. Douglas Wilder became the first black man to be elected governor of an American state. That the state was Virginia, formerly of the Confederacy, lent special significance to the election.

Several of America's most significant and popular historic sites are in Virginia: the Jamestown settlement, Colonial Williamsburg, George Washington's Mount Vernon, Thomas Jefferson's Monticello, and many Civil War battlefields. More humorously, a popular coffee mug proclaims, "To be a Virginian either by Birth, Marriage, Adoption, or even on one's Mother's side, is an Introduction to any State in the Union, a Passport to any Foreign Country, and a Benediction from Above."

Virginia has indeed sought to be a bastion for the ideals that have guided the American nation. Crimes are violations of those ideals. The chapters that follow explain how some violent events throughout Virginia's history have called into question the ideals that Virginians have tried to live by. I will not try to force the crimes into a Procrustean bed to fit a thematic framework—yet this contrast between what Virginians hope for and what the crimes reveal is striking. The first events I will examine occurred in the early days of the new American republic and seemed to justify the fears of the Founders (especially Jefferson) that the next generation might not be ready to lead. In the time of segregation, the 1940s and 1950s, Virginia avoided great racial violence, but the case of the Martinsville Seven pointed out racial disparities in what Virginians had felt was proper justice. In the later 1900s, the death of Sasha Bruce seemed a cruel contrast to the public service practiced by her family. The case of Timothy Spencer cast Virginia justice as progressive and scientific, but later cases did not live up to this lofty standard.

The crimes do not nullify the ideals of Virginians. As Faulkner states, Virginia has been a model and a leader. Virginians have held themselves to lofty standards throughout history. The crimes were occasions to re-examine and to refortify those standards in the face of challenges.

CHAPTER 1

The Case of
Nancy Randolph,
1792–93

On April 28, 1793, Thomas Jefferson wrote to his daughter Martha Randolph.

> A paper which I saw some time ago in the Richmond gazette under the signature of R. R. proved to me the existence of a rumor, which I had otherwise heard of with less certainty. It has given me great uneasiness because I know it must have made so many others unhappy, and among these Mr. Randolph and yourself. Whatever the case may be, the world is become too rational to extend to one person the acts of another . . . I am in hopes therefore that neither of you feel any uneasiness but for the pitiable victim, whether it be of error or of slander. In either case I see guilt but in one person, and not in her. For her it is the moment of trying the affection of her friends, when their commiseration and comfort become balm to her wounds. I hope you will deal them out to her in full measure, regardless of what the trifling or malignant may think or say. Never throw off the best affections of nature at the moment when they become most precious to their object . . .

The rhetoric is nearly biblical: that one becomes noble by giving comfort to the besieged and maligned. Martha had married into the vast Randolph family, and two of her in-laws had been accused of infanticide. Jefferson urges sympathy for the woman in the case, who was the sister of Martha's husband. The accusations against Richard Randolph, "R. R." in Jefferson's letter, led to a hearing at which the defense attorneys were Patrick Henry and John Marshall, quite an impressive team.

The case has fascinated writers since then for its lurid aspects and for the stature and eccentric personalities of the people involved. Along with Jefferson, Patrick Henry, and Marshall, the case engulfed, among others, Virginia politician John Randolph of Roanoke and New York patriot Gouverneur Morris. The case did not end with the hearing; years later alternate versions emerged. These competing accounts, spread across time, make the truth of what occurred nearly impossible to obtain.

Retellings of the case rely on a few contemporary sources. Only a short summary record of the hearing exists, but we have Marshall's extensive file, which describes what the witnesses claimed and includes Marshall's analysis of the evidence. Several of the people involved wrote letters that have survived. Principally, two letters from 1814 and 1815 provide alternate versions to the theory offered in Marshall's notes. The case lives on mostly in chapters in biographies of Marshall, Henry, and the Randolph family. Alan Pell Crawford weaves the original documents and letters into his book *Unwise Passions* (2000), which restored the case to modern attention. The following narrative relies on the contemporary documents and on Crawford.

The Players

William Randolph settled along the James River in the later 1600s. He extended his landholdings and his wealth, and he used his family's associations with the English royal family to influence local affairs. He sired nine children, seven of them sons. The Randolphs spread across Virginia. Jefferson's mother was a Randolph, and Marshall could trace his lineage back to William. So many Randolphs were available that they were willing to marry their cousins. Thus Martha Jefferson, the granddaughter of a Randolph, married Thomas Mann Randolph, a somewhat distant cousin. As we shall see, the cousins need not have been distant to be eligible for marriage.

John Randolph of Matoax (1742–75) had three sons who are pivotal to our story: Richard, born in 1770; Theodorick, born in 1771; and John, called "Jack," born in 1773. Grandson of William, John owned several plantations. In 1790, Richard took over management of the plantation named Bizarre, located along the Appomattox River near Farmville. No source sufficiently explains the name, though the French root of "bizarre" means fantastic or striking, maybe in a good way. Richard's stepfather, St. George Tucker, who would become a prominent judge, wanted Richard to practice law in Farmville. But Richard considered the details of founding a practice and hustling clients too bothersome; he preferred being master of the estate.

He had at his side his wife, Judith, who was also his first cousin, whose brother married Martha Jefferson. Judith's mother resisted the marriage; she wrote to Tucker, "at sixteen and nineteen [the ages of Judith and Richard] we think everybody perfect that we take a fancy to; the Lady expects nothing but condescension, and the Gentleman thinks his Mistress an Angel. . . [but the lovers] are apt to sour when the delirium of love is over, and Reason is allowed to reascend her Throne." Yet the young people insisted.

At Bizarre, the couple soon took in Judith's sister Ann Cary Randolph, called "Nancy." Judith and Nancy's mother had died before Judith's wedding, and their father had married again, choosing a woman not much older than his teenage daughters. Nancy could not abide her stepmother, so Richard offered her a haven. Theodorick, who left college and had become sickly, also sought refuge at Bizarre. Jack later dismissively described Theodorick: "Of all things in the world, he detested most a book. Devoted to pleasure and fun . . . In two years he had undermined his constitution and destroyed his health forever." Theodorick's illness is unclear; some modern writers suggest tuberculosis. Jack, who had to leave the College of William and Mary after fighting a duel (no one was killed), also frequently visited Bizarre. Theodorick and Jack both courted Nancy, as did other cousins. Nancy chose Theodorick, though he was clearly in severe decline. He died on February 14, 1792, before they could marry.

The Crisis

The crisis occurred on the night of September 30, 1792, and the youth of the people involved is striking. Richard was twenty-two, Nancy just seventeen, and Jack nineteen. As twenty-first century readers know, the late-adolescent brain is still forming, especially the brain sectors that weigh responsibility and consequence. The impetuousness of youth probably caused much of what happened.

Richard, Judith, Jack, and Nancy traveled by carriage to the plantation Glenlyvar (sometimes spelled "Glentivar"). The hosts were yet more cousins, Randolph Harrison and his wife, both in their early twenties. Mrs. Harrison's brother, Archibald Randolph, was visiting also and hoped to woo Nancy. Nancy, however, felt unwell and took to bed. The house was still being constructed, so the hosts put their guests in available upper rooms: a big room for Judith and Richard, with a smaller one for Nancy, accessed only through the big room.

Something happened in the smaller room. According to John Marshall's file, the Harrisons claimed that they heard screams in the night coming from Nancy's room. Going to try to help, Mrs. Harrison found the door to Nancy's room bolted. Richard, who was in Nancy's room, eventually let her in, bidding her not to bring a candle lest the light hurt Nancy's eyes. Two slave girls, about ages fifteen and seven, were in the room. After Nancy regained her composure, Mrs. Harrison left. Later, the Harrisons heard heavy footsteps on the stairs, coming down and soon going back up. They assumed that the footsteps were Richard's. During the ensuing days, Nancy kept to the room. On visiting her, Mrs. Harrison noted stains on the pillows and on the stairs; after Nancy left, Mrs. Harrison saw smudged stains incompletely washed from the bedclothes. She took the stains to be blood. Throughout the events, Judith was unworried and explained Nancy's spell as hysteria.

The group stayed a few days longer, then returned to Bizarre. The Harrisons themselves went to Bizarre three weeks later. They told Marshall that they "saw no appearances which might not be accounted for, without ascribing them to an improper cause . . . there appeared to be entire harmony between Mr. Randolph and his lady."

However, both Harrisons told how their slaves reported that Nancy had delivered or miscarried, and "that the Birth had been deposited on a pile of shingles between two Logs, & about six or seven weeks afterwards, he [Mr. Harrison] saw such a place, where there was a shingle which appeared to have been stained." The nasty interpretation was that Richard had discarded the body, and given the configuration of the rooms, he had to carry the bloody bundle past Judith. When the Harrisons heard the story from the slaves is not clear. Whatever their suspicions, the Harrisons' return visit and their quietness about the events might have forestalled any bad reports—if not for the slaves. Others were at Glenlyvar as well and may have gossiped. But it was the slaves who told Mr. Harrison about key evidence and kept the story alive. Slaves could not testify against whites, so whatever the two girls saw in Nancy's room and other slaves saw on the shingles could not come into court. Patricia Brady, in reviewing Crawford's book, finds the role of the slaves fascinating: "Barred from serving as witnesses, they appear to have judged the case among themselves, made that judgment widely known, and used the court of public opinion effectively to ruin the reputations of their 'superiors.'"

As for the pile of shingles, Marshall wrote what he would argue in court: "The story of the shingles has no weight. Had the fact been as supposed, no person on earth would have deposited the birth on a pile of shingles." Unless Richard was too wary to take time at night to bury the body and thus risk discovery, so he left the body in the open and hoped for excarnation—that animals would take it for food.

Whatever their origin, rumors swirled. They focused on Richard, both as adulterer and killer. A letter from Nancy to Judge Tucker, written much later, suggests that Richard procured a statement from Nancy that absolved him, but somehow put her own honor into question regarding her relations with Theodorick. According to this letter, Nancy's brother, Jefferson's son-in-law, threatened Richard never to besmirch Nancy's honor, or "I will wash out with your blood the stain on my family." Richard consulted with Tucker and decided on a preemptive strike. On March 29, 1793, he published a challenge in the newspaper, referenced in Jefferson's letter at the start of this chapter, attesting to his and Nancy's innocence and daring his accusers to present themselves and their evidence. He offered to appear at the county courthouse and allow himself to be arrested, if evidence was forthcoming. Regarding Nancy, he wrote, "Let not a pretended tenderness toward the supposed accomplice in the imputed guilt, shelter me. That person will meet the accusations with a fortitude of which *innocence alone is capable*." When he arrived at the courthouse at the appointed time, he was arrested and jailed pending a hearing.

Youthful impetuousness may explain why Richard would dare people to charge him with a capital offense. Another factor is honor. No warrant or indictment yet existed to charge him with a crime, yet he could not abide a whispered scandal. He had to reply. For him and many Southerners of his time, honor and reputation were not puffy abstractions but treasured commodities. Also, he may have seen Nancy's statement as his insurance, that if the worst happened, he could save himself. Nancy's brother appealed to Richard's honor and his fear to make sure that Richard would never use this insurance. Richard adopted a strategy of total innocence for both him and Nancy. To enact this strategy in court, he sought the best legal talent available, Patrick Henry and John Marshall. (Another attorney, Alexander Campbell, was also involved, mainly to get a deposition from Judith.)

The Hearing

The Order Book of Cumberland County Court briefly states that on April 29, 1793, sixteen justices gathered "for the examination of Richard Randolph who stands committed and charged with feloniously murdering a child said to be born to Nancy Randolph . . . Sundry witnesses were sworn and examined touching the premises and the prisoner heard in his defence." Several comments on this passage are warranted. The phrasing means that the panel examined the evidence and heard the defense's case, not that they heard directly from Richard, as the rules of the time forbade the defendant from speaking to the court. The document lists Richard as the only defendant, not Nancy. And the charge is murder, not inducing an abortion. Indeed, in this era, abortion was not a crime. Supreme Court Justice Harry Blackmun wrote the following in the *Roe v. Wade* decision (1973): "It is perhaps not generally appreciated that the restrictive criminal abortion laws in effect in the majority of States today are of relatively recent vintage. . . It is thus apparent that at common law, at the time of the adoption of our Constitution, and throughout the major portion of the nineteenth century, abortion was viewed with less disfavor than under most American statutes currently in effect." The legal theory behind the arrest was that after Nancy gave birth, that Richard killed the child.

No documents mention a prosecutor. The most likely explanation is that this proceeding was a hearing at which local magistrates heard evidence. The magistrates themselves took the lead in examining witnesses. If they found the defendant guilty, the next step would be a full trial with a jury. (The following chapter will discuss similar proceedings in Richmond's Hustings Court. Indeed, Richard may have faced his county's Hustings Court.) What occurred may be akin to a modern grand jury hearing, with the major difference that in 1793, the defense could present and cross-examine witnesses.

Relatives comprised much of the witness list, among them Martha Jefferson Randolph, who said that Nancy had asked about gum guaiacum, derived from tree resin, which was a cure for colic but also could cause abortion. She added that she assumed Nancy to be pregnant; thus Martha voiced her suspicions against Nancy instead of following her father's advice to comfort the "pitiable victim." A busybody cousin, Mrs. Mary Page, also in her twenties, testified that she suspected Nancy of being pregnant, had overheard conversations between Nancy and her slave about Nancy's growing size, and had even spied through a door crack to watch Nancy undress. Marshall's notes must have been made to prepare for the hearing, because they lack account of what famously happened when Mrs. Page testified. According to Patrick Henry's biography,

Henry had despised Mrs. Page's father and found a way to get back at the family and to neutralize her testimony. He asked her, "Madam, which eye did you peep with? . . . Great God, deliver us from eavesdroppers!" (We all should hope that this really happened.) Family members also spoke of how Richard and Nancy were very fond of each other and much in each other's company; the implication was that Richard was the child's father. The somewhat jealous Archibald Randolph and his friend were among those who so testified. The Harrisons also told their stories.

Marshall offered Jack as rebuttal to these accounts. Jack cooperated fully in his version: Nancy "continued to dress in her usual way: he was much with her; frequently lounged on the bed with her and his Sister [sister-in-law Judith], & never suspected her of being pregnant." Rather than being larger, he found her "pallid & emaciated." Henry also obtained from Judith assurances that "a child could not have been born or carried out of the Room without her knowledge. That she is confident no such event happened."

Marshall's notes express five points for the defense. They focus on Nancy, on the theory that if he convinced the magistrates that Nancy was not pregnant, then Richard could not be guilty of infanticide. First, Richard simply and naturally showed Nancy kindness, especially after Theodorick's death. Nothing untoward happened between them; Judith so attested. Second, the evidence of Nancy's size was inconsistent. And had she been near in time to delivery, her size could not have been hidden. Third, the medicine she asked for had other purposes, and that she eventually got it from Martha Randolph showed that Nancy was not hiding her use of it. Fourth, other sicknesses could explain Nancy's screams and the blood at the Harrisons' home. Fifth, that Nancy refused to let Mrs. Page see her naked was no proof of guilt (especially after Henry humiliated Mrs. Page in court).

The magistrates agreed. Richard was found not guilty.

The Decline

On July 28, 1794, the Cumberland County Order Book records that Patrick Henry sued Richard for nonpayment of the fee for defending him. The Court ruled in Henry's favor. This lawsuit reflects Richard's inevitable troubles with responsibility, both personal and monetary.

Richard and Judith had two sons. Richard took sick and died in June 1796; he was barely twenty-six years old. In his will, he ordered his slaves freed once the family had retired the mortgage on the properties.

Jack, the sole surviving son, tried to manage the family's land-holdings and financial affairs. He had grown into a man who did not look manly. His long legs stretched out of proportion with his torso, giving him an awkward, stilt-like appearance. His facial features never hardened, and his cheeks grew only the faintest stubble. His voice remained high-pitched and adolescent. He wooed at least one other woman besides Nancy, but she too rebuffed him. His enemies wondered if he could perform sexually. He later told his nephew that he suffered from a fever in his late youth that caused these effects; modern analysts have suggested an endocrine imbalance. Despite his odd appearance, he became a successful politician, being elected to the House of Representatives in 1799, when he was only twenty-five. When he presented himself at the Capitol, the Speaker of the House asked if he were old enough to serve. "Ask my constituents," Jack retorted. A fervent and vocal supporter of Jefferson, Jack became a major force in Congress during the early 1800s.

Judith and Nancy, meanwhile, endured a tense and then fractious relationship. Nancy, still perhaps feeling the effects of the scandal, cloistered herself at Bizarre, but saw herself turning into a servant rather than a treasured guest. An ungenerous interpretation is that Richard and Judith sheltered Nancy at Bizarre to protect their own reputations. If they put her out, that act would signal Judith's belief that Nancy and Richard had committed adultery. The sisters maintained an uneasy truce until 1805. That year, when Jack returned to Bizarre from Congress where he led the prosecution (bungled the prosecution, his detractors said) in the impeachment of Supreme Court Justice Samuel Chase, he confronted Nancy and ordered her to leave the estate. A dozen years had passed since the hearing.

Jack himself quarreled with Judith and decamped in 1810 to settle at another Randolph estate, Roanoke. He began to sign his name as "John Randolph of Roanoke," thus separating himself from the home plantations of his father (Matoax) and brother (Bizarre).

Whether from pride or animosity, Nancy did not rely on her relatives nor on Richard's stepfather, Judge Tucker, with whom she maintained consistently good relations. She first went to her ancestral plantation, Tuckahoe, which had been abandoned. Later in Richmond, in an impoverished condition, Nancy met with Jack, but she refused help when days later her nephew brought her money. She went north and found herself in such straits that she did write to Jack for money. He did not reply. She ended up in New York City, in a boardinghouse. She knew one person in the city, so she wrote to him, asking to meet him again. This person was Gouverneur Morris.

Gouverneur Morris

Born in 1752 at his family's estate of Morrisania along the Harlem River, Morris drew favorable attention as an ardent patriot in New York's legislature during the Revolution. Under the Articles of Confederation, he directed the financial office for the thirteen states. He represented Pennsylvania as a delegate to the Constitutional Convention; historians credit him as the chief author of the actual wording in the Constitution.

Morris had met Nancy in the 1780s when he had visited with Virginia patriots, and he had spent enjoyable time at Tuckahoe, becoming impressed by the well-read and well-spoken Nancy. In 1808, he renewed their acquaintance at the boardinghouse and expressed his need for a woman to bring order to his mansion. He offered Nancy not a handout, but a job. He corresponded with her while he traveled, and in April 1809, established her at Morrisania to oversee the housekeeping. According to his reputation, the bachelor Morris enjoyed being with women, but he assured Nancy in a letter that his relations with housekeepers had always been honorable. He pledged, "I will love you as little as I can."

Crawford throughout *Unwise Passions* artfully contrasts Jack and Morris. As a politician, Morris sought compromise and focused on getting results; Jack was an ideologue who broke with President Jefferson and quarreled constantly with his party colleagues. He fought a duel with Henry Clay (both men lived). Tall and robust, though with a pegleg due to a carriage accident, Morris savored a succession of intellectual, lively mistresses; odd-looking and often unpleasant, Jack had no success with women. Morris possessed a self-deprecating humor. When he lost reelection to his Senate seat, he quipped, "My political enemies have had the goodness to relieve me, and although from their motives I cannot be thankful, yet I must be permitted to rejoice in the event." Jack perfected the slashing insult. He coined the infamous put-down, first directed at a New York politician, "like rotten mackerel by moonlight, he shines and stinks." He dismissed the architecture of the Senate chamber as "corn stalk columns and corn-cob capitals." But mostly, the two differed in their regard for Nancy. Morris became her protector; Jack sought to do her harm.

On December 2, 1809, Morris wrote to Supreme Court Chief Justice John Marshall to ask about Nancy's past. He declined to explain how Nancy came to work for him: "it is needless to relate and would be irksome, because it would involve the Necessity of speaking a little too much of myself and have the Air of asking Applause, or at least Approbation." (The line still manages to credit him for helping a person in need, while seeming to avoid credit.) He asked for her "Reputation" and "Standing" in Virginia, and justified the request by saying that he wanted to be sure his association with her would not bring scandal to him as a Federalist Party member. Marshall replied that he did not want to add to Nancy's "afflictions," and that the most convincing fact in Nancy's favor was "that the sister who had the fairest means of judging the transaction, & who was most injured by the fact if true, continued to treat her with an affection apparently unabated, & to afford her an assylum not only during the life of her husband, but long after his death." Marshall thus offers the most favorable reading of Nancy's tenure at Bizarre.

What exactly Morris knew about Nancy's past is only conjecture. He may have known a great deal, for when more odious charges emerged, he still supported Nancy. The measured (and naive?) words of the Chief Justice gave him whatever assurance he needed. At Christmas dinner two weeks after Marshall's letter, Morris shocked his guests by having his brother-in-law, a minister, perform the wedding for him and Nancy. He soon wrote of the nuptials to Marshall: "She had most of the Qualities I wished in a Wife, viz. Good Sense, Good Temper, and Cleanliness. Her Knowledge of House Keeping, which makes the fourth Requisite, was not ample . . . On Beauty I lay no Stress, but, if I did, she has her Share." Morris was fifty-seven; Nancy was thirty-five. The dumbfounded (and probably distraught) wedding guests included Morris's nieces and nephews, who had hoped to inherit his estate. The marriage frustrated their plans. Their frustration deepened in 1813 when Nancy and Morris had a son and heir, Gouverneur Morris II.

Morris continued his life of public service, in 1810 becoming one of the commissioners for the Erie Canal. The following year, the Morrises visited Washington. Such was the arc of Nancy's life that she was born on a plantation, visited Vice President Jefferson at Monticello as late as 1799, became destitute and homeless, then in December 1811 joined her husband as guests of President and Mrs. Madison at the White House.

The Duel of the Letters

In 1814, Richard's son Tudor, age eighteen, a student at Harvard, reestablished contact with Nancy, largely to ask for money. He arranged to visit Morrisania in the fall, but once there collapsed, bleeding from his mouth. The diagnosis was a serious lung ailment. The Morrises cared for him in their home and wrote to Judith and Jack that they should come quickly to Tudor's bedside.

Tudor improved in the interim, and the arrivals of Judith and Jack allowed for tender reunions, at least between Nancy and Judith. For a time, Tudor stayed at Morrisania, and his mother left for home. Jack stayed in New York, and eventually Tudor joined him.

Despite having witnessed the Morrises' kindness to his nephew, Jack nevertheless prepared to spew venom. Physical pain and drugs may have exacerbated his animus: On the way to New York, Jack tumbled down a flight of stairs at an inn, and in New York his coach had overturned. An earlier accident had introduced him to opium, which he took liberally. Further, he had met with David Bayard Ogden, Morris's nephew, who had used loans from his uncle to fund bad investments, who coveted Morris's wealth, and who had no use for Nancy. Jack intertwined Ogden's complaints with his own indictments.

Jack sent the Morrises a letter, dated October 31, 1814, addressed to Nancy.

> You represented to Mr. Morris that I had offered you marriage. Your inveterate disregard of truth has been too well known to me for many years to cause any surprise on my part on this or any other falsehood that you may coin to serve a turn.

He writes a new account of the night in Glenlyvar.

> Your hands had deprived of life that of which you were delivered in October, 1792, at R. Harrison's. The child, to interest his feelings in its behalf, you told my brother Richard (when you entrusted him the secret of your pregnancy and implored him to hide your shame) was begotten by my brother, Theodorick, who died at Bizarre of a long decline the preceding February. You knew long before his death (nearly a year) he was reduced to a mere skeleton; that he was unable to walk; and that his bones had worn through his skin. Such was the inviting object whose bed (agreeably to your own account) you sought . . . His [Richard's] hands received the burthen, bloody from the womb, and already lifeless. Who stifled its cries, God only knows and you. His hands consigned it to an uncoffined grave. To the prudence of R. Harrison, who disqualified himself from giving testimony by refraining from a search under a pile of shingles, some of which were marked with blood—to this cautious conduct it is owing that my brother Richard did not perish on the same gibbet by your side.

Jack piles on more charges: that Nancy was intimate with slaves, that she engaged in prostitution, that she may have killed Richard. Upon seeing her at Morrisania, Jack wrote:

What do I see? A vampire that, after sucking the best blood of my race, has flitted off to the North, and struck her harpy fangs into an infirm old man. To what condition of being have you reduced him? Have you made him a prisoner in his own house that there may be no witness of your lewd amours, or have you driven away his friends and old domestics that there may be no witnesses of his death?

He closes with the desire that Morris will somehow discover what she really is.

The unflappable Morris planned no reply. He had expressed earlier, to Marshall, his distaste for how the Randolphs had scorned and abused Nancy. Nancy, however, would not be silent. Her reply, dated January 16, 1815, begins by saying that Morris has just shown her Jack's letter. But she had clearly brooded over her response, both its content and how to broadcast it. Her letter is three times the length of Jack's, and she sent out twenty copies to his political opponents. The dispute would be public.

She constantly makes fun of his new appellation, "John Randolph of Roanoke." She reminds him that he kissed her at Morrisania: "Did you believe that you held in your arms, that you pressed to your bosom, that you kissed the lips of, a common prostitute, the murderess of her own child and of your brother?"

Nancy reminds Jack that not only did he court her, but that he did so by defaming his own brother Theodorick. "The defamation of your brother whom I loved, your stormy passions, your mean self-ishness, your wretched appearance, rendered your attentions disagreeable. Your brother, Richard, a model of truth and honor, knew how much I was annoyed by them."

She now admits that she was pregnant, by Theodorick, and "We should have been married, if Death had not snatched him away a few days after the scene which began the history of my sorrows." If they had intercourse shortly before his death, the months do work out, as Theodorick died in February, and the visit to Glenlyvar was at the very end of September. She continues that Richard knew and protected her; he was "that most generous and gallant of men."

You have revived this slanderous tale in the most populous city in the United States. For what? To repay my kindness to your nephew by tearing me from the arms of my husband and blasting the prospects of my child!

Nancy then makes a fascinating political charge: that Jack did not fulfill Richard's will to free Richard's slaves because Jack's constituents would object. This charge may have stung deeply; in his own will, Jack did free his slaves. Nancy closes by referencing Shakespeare, declaring Jack's letter to be "a tale told by an idiot, full of sound and fury, signifying nothing."

People today seldom write missives of such eloquent intensity and malice. The 1922 biography of Jack prints both letters in full, and they make good reading. (The author of the biography is William Cabell Bruce, whose granddaughter died in mysterious circumstances that will be discussed in a later chapter.)

Outcomes

The letter did not damage Jack politically. Previously, Jefferson's other son-in-law, John Wayles Eppes, had moved to the district to run against Jack and did defeat him. In the election after Nancy sent the letter, Jack won the seat back. Eventually, he allied himself with Andrew Jackson.

Jack died in 1833. Many of his slaves, freed in his will, moved in a group to Ohio, and their families maintained a proud identity as the descendants of those manumitted by John Randolph of Roanoke. Judith had died in 1816.

Morris also died in 1816. His urinary passage had become blocked, and the tough Morris tried to clear the blockage by inserting a whale bone to puncture it. He did not succeed, instead fatally cutting his internal organs.

Nancy took control of the Morris family's finances and eventually retired the debts brought on by Ogden, who later committed suicide. She sued the coexecutor of the estate for not consulting her and earned full authority. By her death in 1837, the estate had prospered and her son was a man of means. Surprisingly, or not, he chose his mate as a Virginian would: He married a Randolph, his first cousin, the daughter of Nancy's sister Virginia.

What do we know about that night in Glenlyvar? The letters explode Marshall's defense and admit that Nancy did give birth. Was the child stillborn or killed at birth? If killed, was it by Nancy, Richard, or both in conspiracy? The months work out for Theodorick to have been the father, but he was extremely ill in the weeks before his death. Could the child have been Richard's? Crawford emphasizes that Nancy praised Richard throughout her life. In an 1822 letter, she referred to the malady affecting Richard's elder son, Tudor's brother St. George, who was deaf and mute: "What the father attempted visited on the child." Crawford interprets the cryptic line to mean that Richard sought silence about the events of the night in Glenlyvar.

CHAPTER 2

The Death of
George Wythe, 1806

On June 14, 1806, President Thomas Jefferson, mourning the death of his mentor, George Wythe, wrote:

> His advanced years had left us little hope of retaining him much longer, and had his end been brought on by ordinary decays of time and nature, altho' always a subject of regret, it would not have been aggravated by the horror of his falling by the hand of a parricide . . . He was my antient master, my earliest & best friend; and to him I am indebted for first impressions which have had the most salutary influence on the course of my life. I had reserved with fondness, for the day of my retirement, the hope of inducing him to spend much of his time with me.

Jefferson used *parricide* as a general term: A member of Wythe's family had been accused of his murder.

Jefferson felt deep personal debt and affection for Wythe, and he represented the feelings of the leadership of the Commonwealth of Virginia. Wythe was a member of the pantheon of patriots, the great leaders of the Revolution. People recoiled in horror that such a beloved and benevolent personage could be murdered. Through four proceedings, the accused killer was held for trial. But at the trial, the

17

result was a swift acquittal. This curious result has boggled historians for over two hundred years. An explanation may be one that
twenty-first century readers understand: Differing and tentative
medical experts confused the jurors so that they could not render a
guilty verdict. Or the explanation for the verdict may lie in the racial
politics of the time, perhaps in matters of race and testimony, or perhaps in a question of inheritance.

By 1806, at age eighty, George Wythe had become a venerable
figure, and he was continuing his active service to Virginia. Born in
a landholding family, Wythe won election to the legislature and
gained prominence as a lawyer. He taught at the College of William
and Mary, where he instructed Thomas Jefferson. Jefferson read law
in Wythe's office for four years, an unusually long apprenticeship
that demonstrates the bond between the two men. Seventeen years
younger than Wythe, Jefferson revered the older man throughout his
life, as his letter attests. Wythe was an early advocate of a complete
break with Great Britain; he and Jefferson were among Virginia's
delegates to the Continental Congress that declared independence.
With Jefferson and another patriot, Wythe revised Virginia's legal
codes after independence. In 1778, Wythe became one of three
judges on Virginia's Chancery Court, overseeing cases of civil law.
In 1789, he became chancellor, chief officer of that court, and still
held that position at his death. He declined opportunities for national
office to stay in service to Virginia. He taught for decades at William
and Mary. He taught or tutored in his law practice many notable
men: Jefferson, John Marshall, and Henry Clay, whom Wythe took
in as a teenager when Clay's family left Virginia. When he became
chancellor, he moved to Richmond, to Fifth and Grace Streets on
Shockoe Hill, where he died. Perhaps his personal habits account for
his productive longevity: He loved to take daily morning showers,
using very cold water that he drew himself from a deep well.

Wythe outlived two wives, and neither marriage produced children. He doted on his relatives' children and became especially close
to the grandchildren of his sister. Among these was George Wythe
Sweeney, in his late teens in 1806, who had lived with Wythe for
months at a time. Sweeney had no job and no apparent source of

income beyond his family. By all accounts he ran up debts, probably from gambling, many forms of which were rampant in Richmond.

On May 25, 1806, a Sunday, Wythe collapsed into a terrible sickness that lasted until June 8, when he died. Friends who visited described a man weak and in agony. One man later testified that on the first day, Wythe was "confined on his back except when forced up, which was upwards of forty times, and had fifteen large evacuations." Authorities accused Sweeney of poisoning his benefactor.

Sweeney went through four hearings before finally being taken to trial. In the 1950s, W. Edwin Hemphill discovered and published the records of two of those hearings. Those records and the contemporary letters from Wythe's friend and former mayor of Richmond William Duval to Jefferson are the chief sources of information about the events. The record of the trial has never been found. (The burning of courthouses by invading Federals during the Civil War is the usual excuse for missing records.) George Wythe Munford, the son of William Munford, another man tutored by Wythe, published an expanded account in an 1884 book of reminiscences of Virginia history, but his information is somewhat suspect, as we shall see. The following narrative relies on the court records and Duval's letters.

The illness struck Wythe about 9 A.M., after he had taken his coffee and breakfast. The night before, he had eaten strawberries and milk, so he and his visitors wondered about food poisoning, given his symptoms. Doctors who visited suspected cholera. Historian Bruce Chadwick, who has written about the case, considers this misdiagnosis the first of a series of medical mistakes: The gastrointestinal disease cholera might have fit some of Wythe's symptoms, but had not yet been seen in America and the diagnosis likely reflects the doctors' paranoia about epidemics.

On the following two days, May 26 and 27, Wythe's two servants suffered similar symptoms. Both were free people of color. They were Lydia Broadnax, age sixty-six, the housekeeper and cook, who had been with Wythe since he had manumitted her in 1787; and Michael Brown, a teenager of mixed race whom Wythe referred to as a "freed boy" but whose origins are unknown. Earlier in life, in Williamsburg on his family plantation, Wythe had owned slaves. But he gradually divested himself of them, selling some and freeing others. He openly tutored black youths, Michael Brown among them.

On May 27, Sweeney offered to the bank a check for $100 supposedly signed by Wythe. The teller cashed the check, but became suspicious when he finally examined it. After scrutinizing a total of seven checks that Sweeney had recently presented, bank officials showed them to the bedridden Wythe, who denied that he had written them. Authorities charged Sweeney with forgery. After the arrest, Sweeney appealed to Wythe to post bail, and was rebuffed.

On June 1, Michael Brown died. Duval prevailed upon the doctors to perform an autopsy. He wrote to Jefferson of the results: "from the Inflammation in the Stomach & Bowels, they said that it was the kind of Inflammation induced by Poison." The death of Brown spurred significant events. Wythe insisted that his friends search Sweeney's room. There, they found strawberries along with what looked to be arsenic contained in paper packets and a vial.

Wythe altered his will, with four eminent men as witnesses. An earlier version of the will divided the estate among Sweeney and three people of color: Lydia, Michael, and another freed slave who later died. A new revision after that death decreed that Sweeney's share be "charged with debts and demands": Wythe thus showed his awareness of Sweeney's troubles with money. The new version willed Wythe's books to Jefferson and added, "to the said Thomas Jefferson's patronage i [*sic*] recommend the free boy Michael Brown in my testament named, for whose maintenance and other benefit, i will . . . bank stock or the value thereof." A later codicil gave Michael's share to Sweeney should Michael die. On June 1, with Michael dead and Sweeney arrested for forgery, Wythe completely disinherited Sweeney and bestowed his and Michael's previous bequests on Sweeney's brothers and sisters.

Jefferson knew of the earlier will and wrote to Duval mourning for Michael's death, "not only for the affliction it must have cost Mr. Wythe in his last moments, but also as it deprived me of an object for attentions which would have gratified me unceasingly with the constant recollection & execution of the wishes of my friend."

During the following days, Wythe groaned, "Cut me," to several visitors. His speech had become labored and sparse. They thought that he wanted his garments loosened, so they cut his robes. He insistently repeated "Cut me!" and pointed to his chest. They finally took this to be a request for an autopsy after his death. On June 5, he croaked, "I am murdered," though he did not name Sweeney or anyone else as his killer. However, his refusal to post bail for and the disinheriting of Sweeney convey his opinion. George Munford's 1884 account states that Wythe told friends that he forgave Sweeney and did not want him prosecuted. Like many aspects of Munford's version, this point is dubious as it directly contradicts multiple statements by witnesses at the time that Wythe persisted that Sweeney's room should be searched, wanted to be autopsied, and cried out that he was murdered. As he lay dying, Wythe seems to have been ill-inclined toward Sweeney and ordered his friends to seek evidence of foul play. Wythe finally died on June 8.

In tribute to Wythe's influential standing, his casket rested in the House of Delegates for a day. The mourning crossed political lines, and the local newspapers offered lengthy memorials. The state's leading dignitaries attended the funeral, though due to the slow mail Jefferson did not learn of the death until after the burial. Amidst the universal praise for Wythe's character, eulogist and former student William Munford intoned, "It may be said indeed that in one deplorable instance (which it strikes me with horror even to mention), his benevolence was placed on an unworthy object and repaid with *black ingratitude.*"

Meanwhile, the legal system began its dealings with this alleged ingrate on June 2, when Sweeney appeared before the Hustings Court on the forgery charge. On this court, certain city officials acted as justices of the peace; if as a panel they found someone guilty of a serious crime, the case went to a higher court for a full trial. The court took evidence from two bank officials and sent the case to District Court. On June 18, Richmond's mayor and two magistrates held a five-hour hearing and sent Sweeney, now charged with the murders of Wythe and Michael Brown, for another Hustings proceeding. The Hustings panel met on June 23 and sent the murder charges to District Court. Later in the summer, a grand jury issued indictments. Four times, judicial bodies heard evidence and found it sufficient to prove the charges. But none of the four held the ultimate power to decide: Sweeney had to have a trial.

Fortunately, the Hustings Court records survive and tell us what evidence convinced the magistrates. On June 23, fourteen witnesses testified. Two men asserted that Sweeney had discussed poison with them and tried to procure ratsbane, which contains arsenic. A neighbor of the jail said that his servant girl (probably his slave) found in the garden by the jail a paper with a powdery substance inside. The paper was near two broken plants; the witness assumed it was tossed from the jail window. He produced it in court, and officials pronounced the powder to be arsenic based on visual inspection. Sweeney had such a packet on him when he was arrested. Several friends of Wythe described the search of Sweeney's room, and further claimed that Lydia and other black servants had seen Sweeney grinding a yellow substance with an ax and hammer, leaving a residue that the white men testified they had seen. A family friend testified that he had urged Sweeney to reform his life because Wythe's will had provided for him, establishing that Sweeney knew that he was due to inherit Wythe's estate. Further testimony described Wythe's wasted condition, the illnesses of Lydia and Michael, the autopsy on Michael, and finally Wythe's autopsy.

The five doctors who performed the autopsy on Wythe were respected men, not only as doctors but also as political and social figures. Dr. James McClurg, author of a major textbook on stomach bile, a substance that aids in digestion, said, "The whole of his stomach and intestines had an uncommonly bloody appearance, that if produced by arsenic, in his opinion, death would have ensued much sooner." Dr. William Foushee, former mayor of Richmond, said "The stomach was very much inflamed, and appeared as if a new inflammation was coming on. There was very little bile in the liver. The same appearance that his stomach and intestines exhibited might have been produced by arsenic, or any other acrid matter."

Two prominent lawyers took on Sweeney's defense. William Wirt, who later spent sixteen years as U.S. Attorney General, was moving his practice from Norfolk to more populous Richmond and perhaps took the case for the publicity. Edmund Randolph was a bigger surprise, as he had witnessed Wythe sign his final will and had testified to the Hustings Court about the wills and about what the black servants saw in the shed. A former U.S. Attorney General who had fallen from favor, he too may have taken the case for the publicity, to rebuild his legal practice.

Opposing them in court was Virginia's attorney general, Philip Norborne Nicholas. The trial occurred on September 2 and lasted only a day. Sweeney won acquittal for the murder of Wythe; the jury deliberated only "a few minutes" according to the *Richmond Enquirer*. Then the court quashed the indictment for the murder of Michael. The *Enquirer*'s account is very brief and concludes with this paragraph: "The pen yet lingers to add that some of the strongest testimony exhibited before the called court [Hustings] and before the grand jury, was kept back from the petit jury. The reason is, that it was gleaned from the evidence of negroes, which is not permitted by our laws to go against a white man."

Wirt suspected this result as early as June 10. He wrote on that day to James Monroe: "some of those circumstances, material to his [Sweeney's] conviction in a court of law, depend, it seems, on black persons, & so he will escape for the poison." The actual law read as follows: "Any Negro or mulatto, bond or free, shall be a good witness in pleas of the Commonwealth for or against Negroes or mulattos, bond or free, or in civil pleas where free Negroes or mulattos shall alone be parties." That is, blacks could testify *only* against each other. Ironically, a committee including Wythe and Jefferson had reviewed Virginia's laws and left this law intact.

If they could have testified, what would the blacks have said? The notes from Hustings Court relate that whites testified that Lydia and other blacks told them about Sweeney's efforts to grind a yellow substance and about the stained tools that he used, as well as the neighbor who told how his servant found the packet of arsenic in the garden. First, were these men or others allowed to testify to what the blacks had told them? Probably not, as such testimony would be hearsay. But we do not know, as the trial records are lost. Nor can we know for sure why the loss of this information was so fatal to the case, given other significant evidence presented to the Hustings Court—notably the search of Sweeney's room by prominent white men and the substance that looked to be arsenic that they had found there.

As mentioned above, an 1884 book on Virginia history by George Wythe Munford, the son of another Wythe protégé, asserts that Lydia could have given significant testimony. Munford quotes Lydia at length and in vernacular, as if he takes it from recorded testimony. She told how Sweeney went into the kitchen on May 25, got his own coffee, and threw a paper into the fire. After he left the property, Lydia took the coffee and food to Wythe, who asked for his desk keys. She had seen Sweeney with the keys, looking in the desk, where the will was kept. She and Michael drank some of the coffee. In a very short time, all three were sick with cramps. She concluded, "All these things made me think Mars George [Sweeney] must have put something in the coffee-pot. I didn't see him but it looks monstrous strange." Several historians accept this story, including Bruce Chadwick, who incorporates it into his 2009 book *I Am Murdered*.

In a 1955 article, Jeffersonian scholar Julian P. Boyd largely discounts this story on several grounds. First, the contemporary accounts by Duval claim that Lydia and Michael were stricken on the days following, not on the 25th. To Boyd, the dialogue about the will seems contrived. Next, the version is too neat in accounting for motive (the will) and means (the packet of arsenic). Boyd considers it a legend, a version that incorporates the supposedly known "facts" along with the report that blacks could not testify. If Lydia had testified, the legend goes, the whole case would have been resolved.

Another significant indication that "Lydia's story" is fictionalized is that her account appears nowhere in the Hustings Court documents, though other testimony of what whites were told by her and other blacks does appear—about seeing Sweeney use tools to grind a powder. Munford's book claims that she told her tale to Dr. Foushee late on May 25. But when Dr. Foushee testified at Hustings, he never mentioned this version. Probably, he never heard it; probably, Munford created it as a literary device to encapsulate the case.

Yet why was the other evidence, not traced to blacks, insufficient to convict? Chadwick blames the doctors. Using their equivocations in their Hustings testimony, Chadwick asserts that they never definitively ruled Wythe as having died due to arsenic. Though they knew that arsenic was suspected in the death, the doctors did not do sufficient tests for the presence of arsenic, even though such tests were known and uncomplicated to perform. Nor did they examine other areas, such as the eyes and throat, for signs of poison. Instead, according to Chadwick, upon opening Wythe's abdomen they saw conditions that were often related (they thought) to bile, and probed no further. One of them, the expert on bile, may have insisted that his expertise be respected. The fourteen-day duration of Wythe's decline may also have flustered them, for while arsenic poisoning can take days to kill, it seldom takes as long as fourteen days. Their testimony at Hustings was that the malady could have been caused by arsenic, but could also have been another disorder. Chadwick believes that their refusal to be definitive prevented the jury from convicting Sweeney. Chadwick writes that despite their lofty reputations, the doctors were stubborn, ill-informed, and incompetent, and their failure to apply good science (even good observation) led to the acquittal.

Might the doctors have deliberately baffled the jury to give them a means to acquittal? Or might the jury have seen in the medical testimony the excuse for acquittal? Even without the testimony of the blacks and with doctors who refused to speak with certainty, the jury still had plenty of circumstantial evidence, and the verdict remains hard to fathom.

Jack McLaughlin, writing in 1991 about letters to President Jefferson, admits another mystery of the case that few others recognize: "its unanswered questions as to why he [Wythe] would leave much of his estate to a black woman and a mulatto boy." Historian Fawn Brodie ventures into this matter and interprets the verdict as a judgment against Wythe. Brodie's 1974 biography of Jefferson, controversial then and now for its insistent claims that Jefferson did indeed sire children with his slave Sally Hemmings, includes these lines about the Wythe case:

> Jefferson must have surmised, with many others in Virginia once the details of the will were circulated, that Lydia Broadnax was almost certainly Wythe's concubine and Michael Brown his son . . . to ask none other than the President of the United States to be responsible for the boy's education seemed such an obvious advertisement of the boy's paternity that it left many of the citizens of Richmond aghast. . . Thus the whole legal paraphernalia of Virginia law was perverted to absolve the forger and murderer and to dramatize the legal sanction of the murder of a man who would so advertise his miscegenation.

Brodie continues that the acquittal convinced Jefferson that he could not risk "public or legal gesture [of] his acceptance of a yellow child," that is, of Sally Hemmings's children. Eugene D. Genovese, in *Roll, Jordan, Roll: The World the Slaves Made* (1974), discusses several prominent Southerners who lived with slave or free mulatto mistresses and provided in wills for them or their children. If a man were sufficiently wealthy, socially important, and self-secure, he could break the racial taboos. But none of Genovese's examples come from early-1800s Virginia.

Imogene E. Brown battles Brodie's view in her own biography of Wythe, *American Aristides* (1981). She can locate no contemporary charge of miscegenation against Wythe. (The case is much different with Jefferson.) She does find references that Wythe taught at least some of his slaves to write. If Michael Brown was a teenager at his death in 1806, and if Lydia was his mother, Lydia would have been in her late forties or even early fifties when he was born—possible but unlikely. Chadwick cites a study that traces family and tax records; these records never list Lydia as a mother. And no reference to Michael gives his last name as "Broadnax," which would have been the custom.

Wythe was egalitarian in his view of race, and may have taken
Michael into his home as he had taken in Henry Clay, a boy with
immense scholarly potential. Wythe may have made Michael his heir
to explode racial differences, and not necessarily due to paternity.
Perhaps the most effective replies to Brodie are the professions of
esteem from Virginians when Wythe died. Virginia buried him as a
beloved hero, not as a figure of scorn.

Sweeney did not suffer for the forgery charges, either. He was
convicted on two counts. On appeal, Wirt pointed out to the court
that the cited statute concerned frauds between persons and derived
from a time before the founding of banks. Sweeney had defrauded
a bank, and the law as written did not cover such actions. The appellate judges upheld one count regarding the forgeries, but somehow
that conviction also was vacated. The records are unclear on the reasoning. The legislature soon altered the law to make defrauding
businesses a crime.

After the trial, Sweeney disappears from the historical record.
Later nineteenth-century sources claim, without much substantia-
tion, that he went to Tennessee and served time in prison for horse
theft.

Lydia Broadnax appears at least twice more. In April 1807, she
wrote to President Jefferson, reminding him of her long service to
Wythe, telling him that since the poisoning her eyesight had nearly
failed, and requesting his charity. Through his cousin, Jefferson sent
her money; his practice was to use his cousin quietly to distribute
charity. Chadwick uncovered Lydia's will, probated in 1827. She
would have been in her mid–eighties at her death.

CHAPTER 3

Race and the Law: the Martinsville Seven, 1949–51

The Scottsboro case haunted the South. This Alabama case exposed to the nation the ironclad nature of the region's racial prejudice. On March 25, 1931, nine black youths—ages twenty and younger, most of them strangers to each other—boarded an open railroad car. They were living a largely hand-to-mouth existence and were traveling to seek work. A fight ensued with white youths already in the car. The blacks won, and some of the whites abandoned the car. They complained to authorities, who ordered the train to be held at its next stop—Paint Rock, Alabama, near Scottsboro.

When they took the blacks from the car, authorities also discovered two young white women and another white man. The two women claimed that they had been beaten and raped by all the black youths. The women's unbruised bodies and untorn clothes belied their story, as did medical examinations. Yet their story saved them from whatever legal harm might have come to them for riding the rails. The condition of at least two of the boys also belied the women's tale: They were so disabled by disease that they were unlikely to have been able to participate in the attack, especially in the ways the women described. Yet juries convicted all nine and sentenced all but the youngest to death.

Twice the U.S. Supreme Court overturned the convictions: first due to the trial court's failure to appoint specific counsel in a timely manner to allow for preparation of a defense, next due to the absence of blacks' names on the rolls from which jurymen were called. Yet after each overturning, Alabama juries reconvicted and harshly resentenced the defendants. They did so despite the fact that one woman recanted her accusations.

In the view of the national press, the juries ignored evidence, common sense, and justice. In his summation in one of the last trials, attorney Samuel Leibowitz, who had defended the boys for four and a half years, could take no more and railed at the jury. Historian Dan T. Carter narrates the scene:

> Bluntly Leibowitz told the jury he had despaired of convincing a white jury that a Negro accused by a white woman might be innocent. In a voice trembling with anger and fatigue he shouted, "I'm sick and tired of this sanctimonious hypocrisy."

Such was the reaction to the case in the North that when one of the defendants later escaped and was apprehended in Michigan, the governor of Michigan refused to return him to Alabama.

In addition to widespread disdain, the case brought "outside agitators" to the South. The NAACP and a Communist organization vied for control of the defense as a means to publicize their social agendas. When the Communists won the right to provide the defense, they made the case an international *cause celebre*.

By strictly following legal procedures in cases that involved race, Virginia sought to forestall the opprobrium that attached to Alabama because of the Scottsboro case. The Virginia case of the Martinsville Seven compares with Scottsboro in that it attracted national scrutiny and outside agitators. Proud of their adherence to legal forms, Virginia officials resented and resisted the criticisms that descended upon them in connection with the Martinsville case. While the case did expose racial bias in some of Virginia's procedures, the case differed from Scottsboro in the most fundamental way—the evidence for the defendants' guilt.

On the night of January 8, 1949, in Martinsville, near Danville in the southwestern sector of the commonwealth, a thirty-two-year old white woman named Ruby Floyd claimed that she had been seized and raped by a gang of black men. After a short investigation, police arrested seven blacks. All seven were convicted and later executed.

Virginians wanted to point to the case as a triumph of the legal process. Historian Eric W. Rise researched the case extensively and writes, "By diligently adhering to procedural requirements, the court attempted to try the case, in the judge's words, as if 'both parties were members of the same race.'" In many aspects, the case received more careful and professional handling than the Scottsboro defendants received. Yet the case received national attention. This time, the disparity involved sentencings: The case exposed the fact that only blacks received the death penalty for rape.

The following narration relies largely on Eric W. Rise's 1995 book on the case, *The Martinsville Seven: Race, Rape, and Capital Punishment*. About 7:30 on the evening of January 8, in the black section of town, Ruby Floyd banged at the door of Mrs. Mary Wade. Mrs. Floyd was crying, bruised, and muddy; she wore a torn slip with no skirt. She claimed that she had been gang-raped. Taking a gun for protection, Mr. Jesse Wade guided her to a nearby store so that they could telephone police. When police arrived, Floyd told them that she maybe recognized two of her attackers walking on the street; the police arrested them. As the night wore on, the two men confessed, leading to the arrests of five more men.

In both evidence and procedures, this case greatly contrasts the Scottsboro case. Three evidentiary factors are important: the victim, the confessions, and several corroborating witnesses.

Mrs. Floyd and her husband had moved to Martinsville four years before so that he could manage a store. They were Jehovah's Witnesses, and Mrs. Floyd often proselytized in the black community. Thus she may have felt comfortable going into that community at night to collect a small debt. That night, her torn clothing and scratched body matched her account of a violent attack. She claimed that as many as twelve or thirteen men had attacked her; she was too traumatized to be certain. The attacks came in two waves: First she was seized as she was walking and pulled into a field; then she escaped briefly but was dragged back to where other men joined in the assault. When she had nearly escaped, she encountered three people on the way to a bus; she grabbed one of them, a woman, and wrenched off a coat button, but the witnesses did nothing as a man pulled Mrs. Floyd away. Mrs. Floyd said that the attackers held her down, yelled at her to spread her legs, mashed their faces onto hers, and took turns mounting her. Eventually, they let her go. Medical examination right after the events confirmed her account of multiple sexual assaults. She screamed during the exam and had to be sedated. She suffered physical and emotional problems long after these events.

Remarkably consistent confessions verified Mrs. Floyd's story. Of the two men taken into custody based on Mrs. Floyd's tentative identification, one confessed after a witness also identified him. Police told the other man that his companion had confessed, so the second did as well, telling a story that matched the first's in its key specifics. Both stories implicated five other men. Police arrested four of them. The fifth evaded capture for a day and then surrendered after talking to Mrs. Wade, the same woman who had helped Mrs. Floyd. All seven gave confessions. The versions matched in general outline, though differed on how each man described his own responsibility. The story went as follows: A group of four men who had been drinking watched Mrs. Floyd go into the neighborhood. On her way back, they chased and subdued her. Another man went to a nearby house and said that men had a woman by the railroad track. This man and two men from the house went to look and then joined the attack. The callousness of this second group deserves mention.

The men were Howard Hairston, Frank Hairston, Booker T. Millner, and Joe Henry Hampton in the first group; and Francis DeSales Grayson, John Clabon Taylor, and James Luther Hairston in the second. Grayson, who had urged the other two to go see what was happening, was the eldest; in his thirties, he had a wife and five children. The others were in their late teens and early twenties, not well-educated. They were working as laborers, living with their families. Some of them had police records, but nothing suggesting the violence of the rape.

Several witnesses backed up Mrs. Floyd's story. When Mrs. Floyd entered the area that night to collect a debt, she needed directions. A resident whom she asked volunteered her eleven-year-old son, Charlie Martin, as a guide. Charlie witnessed the first group grab Mrs. Floyd, and the attackers shooed him away, giving him a quarter and a knife, according to his testimony. He was the witness whose identification in the jail convinced the first man arrested to confess. Mrs. Ethel Mae Redd testified that Grayson, her lodger, told about the attack and urged two others to go see. And the three people whom Mrs. Floyd approached when she temporarily escaped verified her story. In a terrible irony, one of them was fourteen-year-old Leona Millner, sister of Booker Millner; the woman whose coat button was torn was Josephine Grayson, Grayson's wife. They both had to testify in some of the trials.

The courts carefully followed legal procedure in handling this case. Later in January, Judge Kennon C. Whittle appointed each defendant separate counsel. Among the appointed lawyers was the region's current state senator. With the trials set for late April, the lawyers had time to devise their defenses. Again, these procedures show evolution from those in Scottsboro, where trials were held swiftly with counsel appointed on the day of trial. The grand jury that voted indictments had black members. But at the trials, the juries were all white. Blacks in the jury pool either could not serve because they objected to the death penalty or were struck without comment by the prosecution. Finally, Judge Whittle asked on the record that the lawyers avoid references to race during the trials.

The judge agreed to sever the cases, though two of the defendants chose to be tried together. As a legal tactic, severance necessitated that the state prove each man's specific involvement, and the tactic prevented the state from using the co-defendants' confessions against each other. Severance also required that Mrs. Floyd testify multiple times.

With Mrs. Floyd, the corroborating witnesses, and each defendant's confession, the prosecution had sufficient evidence in each trial. Some defense attorneys were tough on Mrs. Floyd, charging that she could not really identify her attackers and intimating that her poor judgment in going into that area at night made her partly responsible. The defendants variously offered as defenses that they were drunk and not aware of what they were doing and that Mrs. Floyd seemed compliant.

Six trials occurred over eleven days. The trials ended in convictions, with deliberations in each taking under two hours. The juries voted that each defendant should be executed. The defenses had hoped to avoid execution. Drunkenness cannot mitigate guilt, but can mitigate the penalty. It did not here, nor did the lack of previous histories of violence.

For the appeals, once again the NAACP and a group with Communist sympathies vied for control. The Communist group this time was the Civil Rights Congress (CRC) an agency largely focused on racial issues. This group tended to argue for the actual innocence of the men, and the CRC strongly believed in demonstrations, letter-writing campaigns, and media efforts all as ways to mobilize people to action. Much of the outside attention that came to Virginia due to the case resulted from the CRC's efforts.

In contrast, the NAACP, which wrested control of the appeals, worked through the court system. NAACP officials felt sobered by the apparent guilt of the defendants, a key contrast with the CRC. Yet the lawyers saw in the case the chance to make significant legal points about racial discrimination within Southern justice. The chief lawyer for the appeal was Martin A. Martin, a black attorney from Danville who had experience in appeals of capital cases. For the first state appeal, Martin argued that the venue should have been changed, that the trials should not have taken place serially, that the confessions were invalid, and that the jury's composition of only those who supported capital punishment introduced bias. The first three points were obvious ones that most appellate attorneys would have offered. These points were not successful. On the fourth, the team thought they could gain legal traction by expanding the argument that the overwhelming majority of death sentences for rape were given to black defendants.

Martin and his team honed their argument for further appeals with their eyes on federal courts, because they were raising a constitutional issue. They tried out their expansive legal theory first in September 1950 in Virginia's Hustings Court, which had jurisdiction in Richmond, where the defendants were imprisoned. Martin's and his team's presentation highlighted several key points. Prior to the Civil War, by statute in Virginia, only blacks could receive death for the rape of a white woman. Current law had no racial distinction, but current practice did. Since 1908, when the state assumed the power to execute (taking it from localities), forty-five blacks had been executed for rape, and eight more had been so sentenced, but only one white man had received the sentence, and he later was pardoned. (Indeed, a contemporary study based on census records exposed that between 1938 and 1948, 93 percent of the men executed in the South for rape were black.) In Virginia, twice as many blacks as whites received life sentences for rape. Thus, blacks did not receive equal protection in the courts, as guaranteed by the Constitution.

Virginia Attorney General J. Lindsay Almond used the argument of due process rather than equal protection: that is, the legal process in this case was followed correctly and fairly. He emphasized that the facts of this case—the "unspeakable and bestial horror" of gang rape against "a defenseless woman of any color"—deserved the most severe punishment. The juries ruled, he argued, not from racial prejudice but from revulsion at the actual events.

When he issued his ruling denying the appeal, the judge could not see how the juries could be construed as state agents. Referring to the historic cases that Martin had used, the judge wrote, "Certainly 54 different juries sitting over a period of 42 years in localities from all over the state cannot be said to be acting under any concerted action, policy or system for which the state is responsible." Regarding the statistical disparity, the judge wrote that the proper solution was legislative, not judicial.

Through this process, Gov. John S. Battle granted stays of execution to allow appeals to proceed. When Martin's team appealed directly to him for clemency, he held a hearing to allow the defense's views to be heard. Martin made sure that all the speakers were Virginians. But like the courts, Battle refused to intervene, beyond allowing further stays.

Martin exhausted the federal appeals open to him. The Hustings Court ruling was directly appealable to the U.S. Supreme Court, which declined to take the case. Martin then started over with the federal system. He won a hearing in District Court, but after it denied his appeal, he failed to get a hearing at the next level, the Circuit Court of Appeals. In an extraordinary scene, just after midnight on Friday, February 2, 1951, Chief Justice of the U.S. Supreme Court Fred M. Vinson personally heard arguments from Martin and two others for about ninety minutes, but rejected their appeal.

Several hours later, at daylight, four of the Martinsville Seven were electrocuted. The three others were put to death on the morning of Monday, February 5, 1951. The grouping of their executions matched the two groups that attacked Mrs. Floyd.

Reflecting on the case later in life, Governor Battle explained, "I tried to figure out a way to keep a couple of those younger men from being electrocuted. But they were as guilty as the rest . . . I've slept with a clear conscience. The law had spoken." The gruesome specifics of the gang rape and the security in the defendants' guilt had trumped the racial statistics. Yet the statistics that Martin exposed remain appalling, in 1950 and today. Harvard Law Professor Randall Kennedy writes harshly in *Race, Crime and the Law* (1997), "the legal system has shown itself to be largely incapable of acknowledging the influence of racial sentiment in the meting out of punishment even in circumstances in which the presence of such bias is obvious." An issue that seemed to prevent courts from acting on the statistics was the murkiness of the remedy. In Virginia, could courts have vacated the death penalties for blacks convicted of rape yet kept capital punishment available for white defendants, creating a clear disparity? According to Kennedy, in the 1960s, an appellate attorney in Arkansas, using logic similar to that used in Martinsville, expressed willingness to accept such an arrangement. As occurred in Martinsville, in these matters courts rejected the broad statistics and focused on the cases at hand.

The U.S. Supreme Court resolved the issues brought up in Martinsville in *Coker v. Georgia*, 1976, by declaring capital punishment unconstitutional for rape. Kennedy points out that the Court sidestepped the racial statistics: Cases from Georgia involving interracial rape were before the Court, but the Justices chose the case in which both the convicted rapist and the victim were white.

CHAPTER 4

The Death of Alexandra Bruce Michaelides, 1975–81

On November 7, 1975, on the grounds of Staunton Hill, her family's estate in rural Charlotte County, Alexandra "Sasha" Bruce Michaelides suffered a gunshot wound to the temple.

Descendant of an influential family and daughter of a respected diplomat, twenty-nine-year-old Sasha had retreated to the estate after her education at Radcliffe and experience with an art gallery in London. Three months before the shooting, she married Greek businessman Marios Michaelides. Late on the afternoon of the 7th, he roused the tenants on the property to tell them that he had found his wife's body under a cedar tree. She was alive but unconscious. At the hospital, medical staff discovered bruises on her face and body; the gray and yellow coloring showed that some bruises were recent, some older. Two days later, without regaining consciousness, Sasha died. The medical examiner, Dr. Lewis J. Read, conducted no autopsy, largely to comply with her father's wishes, and ruled the death as suicide based on the wound and the statements from Michaelides that his wife had been depressed and had attempted suicide previously.

Anxiety over the death lingered in the Bruce family. In 1976, the parents hired a private detective whose investigation persuaded local authorities to reopen the case. The detective became convinced that Marios Michaelides had looted Sasha's wealth before and after her death and that he should be indicted for murder. The county prosecutor agreed.

The death of Sasha Bruce features what would come to be standard elements of true crime: a prominent family, a troubled daughter, a mysterious suitor, a death under murky circumstances, a relentless and colorful private detective, legal challenges in bringing the case. Three elements make the case especially significant. First is the question of evidence, as various interpretations emerged both of the crime scene and the financial dealings that preceded Sasha's death. Another is the international element: Michaelides was in Greece when Virginia authorities tried to arrest him, and he refused to return, causing great debate over how to proceed. But the most significant element is the unfathomable personality of Sasha Bruce, an intelligent and willful woman who placed herself in vulnerable situations.

The Family

The Bruce family had arrived in America before the Revolution and became wealthy landholders, but they lost their fortune in slaves and property due to the Civil War. Sasha's father, David K. E. Bruce, born in 1898, restored the family's wealth. After a short career in the Maryland legislature, he joined the diplomatic corps and rose to become a trusted ambassador who served presidents of both parties. He was America's ambassador to France, West Germany, and Great Britain (for eight years, a record), then envoy to China (America's first such envoy), then to NATO. He retired in 1976.

He restored the family's wealth by his 1926 marriage to Ailsa Mellon, daughter of financier and Treasury Secretary Andrew Mellon. Andrew Mellon gave Bruce a million dollars, and he used part of it in 1933 to buy back Staunton Hill, the family's 293-acre Virginia estate that his father had sold. Bruce and Ailsa had a daughter, but the couple grew apart and divorced in 1945. He quickly married Evangeline Bell, twenty years his junior, with whom he worked in the Office of Strategic Services, a forerunner of the CIA. Evangeline was the daughter and stepdaughter of diplomats and thus understood the life that Bruce was creating for himself. She earned a reputation as a gracious and literate hostess. She was interested in languages and history, and late in life she wrote a well-reviewed biography of Napoleon and Josephine. She and Bruce had three children, Sasha being the eldest, born in 1946, when Bruce was forty-eight. Two sons, David and Nicholas, followed.

In the early 1970s Bruce became concerned about the disposition of Staunton Hill. He devised a plan to sell the estate to the three children for $100,000, each sibling putting up a third. The children all had access to significant trusts and theoretically could afford the cost, though Sasha, as we shall see, had trouble with her third. Eventually, the children consummated the deal. One brother lived sporadically at the estate, and Sasha would adopt it as her home.

The Troubled Daughter

Sasha's résumé is impressive. She attended boarding school at St. Timothy's outside Baltimore. She graduated from Radcliffe College in 1969, where she specialized in art history. She applied this academic interest at archeological digs in New Mexico, Turkey, and Israel; friends reported that she felt the lure of archeology. In London, she became involved with a gallery that sold medieval icons. Sasha devised shows and catalogs for the gallery and even went to auctions with authority to bid.

The darker aspects of her résumé appear in *Privilege: The Enigma of Sasha Bruce* (1982) by English professor Joan Mellen. From interviews with Sasha's classmates, friends, and coworkers, Mellen creates a portrait of a troubled woman engaged in reckless behavior. In college, Sasha suffered from bouts of depression. She experimented with drugs. She engaged in promiscuity, even seeking out married men, according to Mellen's sources. In London, the owner of the icon gallery, Greek-born Anton Von Kassel, bounced checks, sold forgeries, and eventually went bankrupt. Sasha had propped up the business with her own money and endangered the status of her trusts, and Mellen charges that she had to know about the frauds. Sasha had a long-term affair with Von Kassel, though she knew that he was married. He eventually fled London ahead of creditors and the law. Mellen's thesis is that Sasha craved "disapproval"—she rebelled against the respectability of her family and engaged in behavior that challenged their ideals of propriety and morality. In Mellen's view, Sasha felt minimal self-worth and thus did bad things with bad people—such as facilitating the frauds perpetrated by her married lover. Her next lover, Marios Michaelides, was also married.

Yet Sasha was a woman with at least three significant personal assets—they emerge from the news accounts and from Mellen's book (in subtext). Sasha was remarkably intelligent: Her thesis on the art within a medieval manuscript earned her *magna cum laude* honors from Radcliffe. During her time at Radcliffe, she volunteered significant weekly hours at the Lyman School for Boys, a facility for the poor and wayward. She earned a reputation among the boys as both caring and tough. Appalled by some of the conditions there, she eventually used her father's connections to contact a state official to urge him to investigate. Ambassador Bruce's biography includes this 1968 entry from his diary about her: "Unselfish to a striking degree, she has an almost fierce attachment to her family and a deep sympathy for the unfortunate and dispossessed." Finally, Sasha inspired loyal friendships with both men and women. These friends contacted and visited her until her death.

As Von Kassel's icon business collapsed, Sasha left London and sought respite at Staunton Hill. She may have been fearful that British creditors would seek to hold her partially liable for the frauds. She tried to fit into the rural setting. She became close with the tenants. She raised chickens in an attempt to start an egg business and sought out markets for her eggs, though this venture was ultimately unsuccessful. And she awaited the arrival of Michaelides.

The Mysterious Suitor

Sasha met Michaelides, ironically, at the Greek wedding of Von Kassel's brother, which Sasha attended alone. Within a few weeks, they became a couple. Born in 1945, Michaelides sometimes acted as agent for his family's businesses selling grain and fruit. He also engaged in stock trading. And he was married to Mary Lewis, an American teacher who worked in Greece. When Sasha returned to the United States in 1974, she announced that eventually Michaelides would join her and marry her.

No one connected with Sasha ever told reporters anything good about Michaelides, except that Sasha seemed devoted to him. People could not decipher his source of income. When he met her friends, he was aloof and terse and reluctant to let Sasha talk with them alone. They claimed that he was cutting off her many close friends, isolating her on the estate. Thus a planned visit by her godmother to begin on the day that Sasha suffered the shooting took on significance to her friends; it implied that Sasha was finally acting independently of Michaelides.

Dates tell the story. In a document dated February 24, 1975, Sasha surrendered her portion of Staunton Hill to her brother Nicholas, but Nicholas did not file the transfer until after her death. On July 21, Sasha saw a lawyer and created a will that granted Michaelides all of her personal property at her death, provided that they had married; Michaelides witnessed the creation of this will. On July 25, he and his wife obtained divorce documents from Haiti. At the time, his wife was pregnant, and she gave birth on March 20, 1976. Michaelides acknowledged the girl as his. Back in Virginia on August 8, 1975, Sasha and Michaelides married in a civil ceremony.

Before and after the marriage, Sasha and Michaelides telephoned and visited her bankers to have her accounts put in his name. Michaelides's probable ploy to convince Sasha to do this, according to Mellen, was that the creditors of Van Kassel's gallery might come after her fortune, so that her assets should be in his name for safekeeping. Yet he also took possession of the family's heirloom silver and arranged, in Sasha's presence, to sell off the extensive antique book collection housed at the estate. Mellen records that the proceeds from the books exceeded $50,000, all of it deposited in Michaelides's Swiss accounts.

The Shooting

Friends and family agree that Sasha had withdrawn from them with the arrival of Michaelides. So Sasha's invitation to her godmother and the godmother's friend to spend the weekend at Staunton Hill was a welcome change. On November 7, 1975, the morning of their expected arrival, Sasha prepared a cake and selected wines. Late that afternoon, she was shot in the head.

The weapon was a Walther pistol that belonged to Michaelides and that he told police that he had hidden lest his depressed wife attempt suicide. The shot entered her right temple; for the left-handed Sasha to have shot herself in this way, she would have had to hold the gun awkwardly with both hands. And the authorities had questions about the bruises; Michaelides admitted that he had been physical with her. But when she died two days later, the medical examiner ruled suicide. The family, led by her father, interred her immediately at Staunton Hill. Ambassador and Mrs. Bruce returned quickly to Washington and then to Bruce's NATO posting in Brussels, leaving the brothers to deal with Michaelides.

Some of the family trusts that Sasha accessed were closed to Michaelides due to longstanding restrictions. Michaelides had only tentative rights to the house, and the flurry of agreements among the siblings had complicated the issue of ownership. Somehow, Michaelides and the brothers came to an understanding. On November 20, not two full weeks after Sasha's death, the three visited a lawyer and crafted a document by which Michaelides renounced his claim to Sasha's estate. Early in 1976, the brothers gave him $190,000. Meanwhile, each time Michaelides visited Staunton Hill, ostensibly to take his belongings and mail, he removed Bruce family property.

When Michaelides was indicted for Sasha's murder, people wondered in the press about his motive, reasoning that if he wanted her full estate, he could have sued and argued that he deserved it based on her will from July 21. His renouncing his claim seemed to argue against his being a killer. But, whether or not he killed her, he had already made a lot of money by taking her investments and felt primed to make more from the books and the Bruce antiques that he took. Arguing for his rights according to her will could be over-reaching and dangerous. By this theory, he got what he could and got out while he was not under formal suspicion. The more he pushed for her estate, the more he risked that people might ask about the bruises and the gun. Michaelides's detractors have a theory for why on this day he may have killed her: The pending visit of an outside influence, her godmother, spurred him to action.

The Private Detective

In 1976, Ambassador and Mrs. Bruce hired Downey Rice to investigate Sasha's death. A lawyer who had worked for the FBI and had served as counsel to the Congressional Kefauver Commission that investigated organized crime, Rice was a colorful character. In November 1978, when the Bruce case brought him attention, he regaled Tom Zito of the *Washington Post* with tales of the old days. He died suddenly—of natural causes—within a week of the interview's publication, just as the Bruce case had gotten national attention.

Rice studied the phone records at Staunton Hill, noting the calls to Sasha's financial officials and several to Tennessee, to the home of Michaelides's first wife, Mary. Claiming accurately to be a lawyer for the family seeking to resolve Sasha's estate, Rice traveled to Alabama, the new residence of Mary, and met with her and her ex-husband, with whom she spent much time, and their infant daughter. The couple had named the daughter Mary Alexandra Eugenia Michaelides. Rice strung out negotiations with Michaelides, focusing on whether he owed the estate for a Jaguar that Sasha had given him but that he had wrecked. As he gathered evidence, Rice met with police and prosecutors in Virginia and urged arrest warrants. By early May 1978, he had convinced them.

The warrants were for grand larceny—the thefts of the books—and for bigamy, as Rice had convinced the authorities that the Haitian divorce documents were improper. The bigamy charge was another avenue to recover Bruce family possessions by denying that Michaelides was actually Sasha's husband. On May 8, 1978, believing that Michaelides was in Alabama, Virginia and Alabama police went to where he lived with Mary to arrest him. Mary was there, but Michaelides was in Greece. Mary phoned him to warn him; the police had no legal recourse to stop her. The police did notice items in the home, consulted with the Bruce family, and returned three days later with search warrants for the items that Michaelides had removed from Staunton Hill. In September, police executed another search warrant to recover Bruce property from a nearby warehouse. The items included silver with the family crest, a painting by noted 1800s portraitist Thomas Sully, statues, and antique books.

Spurred by Rice, Commonwealth Attorney for Charlotte County Edwin B. Baker convened a special grand jury. In July the jury issued indictments for bigamy and for the thefts of the books and property. On September 8, the grand jury indicted Michaelides for murder.

International Complications

Greece and the United States lacked an extradition treaty, but Greek law allowed a citizen charged with a crime in another country to be arrested and tried in Greece. In October 1978, the Greek government obligingly charged Michaelides with murder. He would remain free as long as he cooperated with the Greek court.

Michaelides wrote to the Virginia authorities to deny his guilt, to claim that Sasha had given him the disputed Bruce family artifacts, and to attack the Bruce family for mistreating Sasha and for harassing him. He soon offered, via a Virginia lawyer, to return to Virginia for trial if various members of the Bruce family took polygraph tests.

Baker refused to turn over the file of evidence to the State Department so that it could be sent to the Greek court. Baker openly wanted Michaelides tried in Virginia or wanted to be involved in the prosecution in Greece; both were very unlikely to occur. The governor of Virginia, John N. Dalton, tried to negotiate between Baker and the State Department. Not until late 1979 did Baker surrender the file.

In spring 1980, the State Department sent the file, translated into Greek, to Greece. In the Greek system, a judge would review the file and then hear from the accused. Michaelides could comment on the evidence, but in Greece (as in much of Europe) he would be questioned by the judge, unlike the American system in which the defendant is not required to speak. The hearing would determine whether the Greek courts would proceed with the case.

The hearing occurred in March 1981. Michaelides asked Joan Mellen to testify, and she agreed. Eerily, Michaelides's newest female companion translated for her in court. When the judge asked, "What about Marios makes you think he's not a murderer?" Mellen gave her theory that Sasha was a depressed and self-destructive woman and that Michaelides had exacerbated these tendencies. Mellen writes that she testified "that Marios had convinced Sasha she must 'purify herself' to become worthy of him, and how miserable she had become under the enforced isolation he demanded at Staunton Hill." The *New York Times* review of Mellen's book judges that "writers who voluntarily entangle themselves with the characters of a criminal case that they are investigating run the risk of blurring their objectivity or their reputation for objectivity—which amounts to the same thing in journalism."

The Greek court declined to indict Michaelides. Sasha's brother David appealed the decision through the Greek court system, to no avail.

In a 1984 interview with the *New York Times*, Evangeline Bruce stated, "It is resolved in the whole family's mind that she was murdered by her husband."

Legacies

Ambassador Bruce died in December 1977, at age seventy-nine, while Rice was still working on the case. After Sasha's death, he never returned to Staunton Hill. During Rice's investigation, authorities disinterred Sasha's body for autopsy. The medical examiner again ruled suicide. Her remains were cremated and buried in Maryland near the ambassador's grave. Evangeline Bruce lived until 1995. David Bruce, son and brother, established a bed-and-breakfast at Staunton Hill.

In 1976, Evangeline involved herself with an agency that used the basement of a Washington, D.C., church as a drop-in center for troubled youths. Evangeline's donation transformed the agency into Sasha Bruce Youthwork Inc. Evangeline explained to the *New York Times* in 1984 that when as a Radcliffe student Sasha had volunteered at Lyman House she "dealt with some of the same problems that we are trying to cope with now. She found the work fascinating. It was a great subject of conversation in our home." Of this particular organization, she said, "Their spirit was so contagious. They were working with children who were sleeping under the Key Bridge and wandering around Georgetown. What they needed was a facility as a temporary refuge for teen-agers, so we found a little town house and Sasha Bruce House was opened in early 1977." Sasha Bruce Youthwork offers havens to runaways, homeless children, and at-risk teens. It offers group homes, youth employment, legal assistance, and more. By 2010 it provided eighteen programs. Evangeline served as an officer on the board and vigorously raised funds.

Evangeline offered this tribute to Sasha: "For me this work is a way of giving to something that Sasha very much cared about. I think this network for young people would have made her very happy. Of all the things I think she would have chosen, it would have been this."

CHAPTER 5

DNA Comes to America: The Case of Timothy Spencer, 1987–94

"A new biological test promises to change radically the way criminologists track down murderers, rapists, and muggers. Virtually foolproof identification of any person is now believed possible through the powerful new laboratory test that detects genetic 'fingerprints' in tiny samples of blood, semen, and hair roots."

So science writer Lawrence K. Altman began his 1986 article in the *New York Times* about DNA analysis.

His article and others educated the public about the new technology. Scientists had discovered how to isolate genetic material from biological samples, and then how to apply enzymes and radioactivity to a sample to produce an image. This image makes visible each individual's unique genetic makeup. As an image, it can be compared to other images from other samples. (Only identical twins have the same DNA image.) The DNA of children will expose inheritance patterns from parents, so the tests and images can also be used to determine paternity. Scientists managed to harvest genetic material for testing from small samples as well as from samples several years old. The early articles warned that the analysis is time-consuming, often taking weeks.

In 1994, eight years later, a *Washington Post* headline reported, "In Grim Distinction, Va. Killer Is 1st to Die Based on DNA Test." Virginia was indeed the first state to apply the new technology to a capital case. The investigation mixed the technology with insightful police work. Authorities might never have sought full DNA analysis unless a detective had discerned patterns within crimes from different parts of the commonwealth.

The case that first brought DNA technology to the attention of the police occurred in Great Britain in the 1980s. The chief source for the case is the American crime writer Joseph Wambaugh, who researched and described the case in *The Blooding* (1989). In the county of Leicestershire, two fifteen-year-old girls suffered rape and murder as they walked near wooded pathways. The deaths happened almost three years apart, with the first murder occurring in November 1983 and the second in July 1986. In the second killing, the police took into custody a seventeen-year old whom Wambaugh referred to as "the kitchen porter"—he worked at the nearby hospital for the mentally ill. The porter came to the police's attention by telling stories to friends about the body—stories with incorrect information—at a time when no one should have known about the crime. During more than twelve hours of questioning, the boy admitted to violent sex with girls, to attempting to touch very young girls, and eventually to the second killing; his versions of the death seldom agreed with each other and did not match specifics of the scene. Nevertheless, the police charged him with the killing.

Wambaugh writes that the two sides dispute who had the idea of consulting Dr. Alec Jeffreys, a thirty-some-year-old geneticist at Leicester University whose research had begun to appear in the popular press. Jeffreys had managed to isolate DNA into molecular fragments and then apply radioactivity; the process yielded images of bands and patterns. Wambaugh writes, "The distribution of these bands would be unique, person to person, and so they [the researchers] would be looking at a DNA image that would be individually specific." The team tested bodily fluids and discovered that if the fluids came from the same individual, the DNA patterns would be identical. Thus, a blood sample and a semen sample from the same donor would match and would do so across time. Jeffreys could also trace DNA contributions from parents. He presented his findings to scientists and wisely patented his discovery. The earliest applications of his new technology beyond the lab involved paternity and immigration disputes.

The porter's father, believing that his backward son could not be a killer, requested that his son's DNA be compared to the deposit left on the second victim. The police had different motives for requesting a DNA test: They asked for DNA comparisons of the porter against the deposits from both murders because they hoped to charge him with the earlier death. For whichever reason, Jeffreys was called into the case. Jeffreys personally told the police that the porter was not a match with either crime, but that the deposits from both crimes did match. The police were tracking one killer, Jeffreys concluded, but that killer was not the porter.

Two aspects deserve attention here. First, Wambaugh records Jeffreys as speaking with surety: The porter is innocent; the same man killed both girls. In the decades since, researchers have tended to speak in probabilities and statistical matches, avoiding the definitive. But Jeffreys and Wambaugh can be forgiven for their enthusiasm over the new technology. The second is much more sobering: Were it not for the DNA evidence, a seventeen-year-old boy with a troubled personality, held in custody and questioned for more than twelve hours, who gave a confused confession, could have been found responsible for murder. The DNA rescued him. This conflict of science versus interrogation repeated itself in Virginia.

The police decided to ask each male in the community within a generous age range to submit to DNA testing to exclude him as a suspect. Each man would be "blooded," the English term for using a needle to collect a blood sample. Remarkably, the men of the community largely complied, and the police blooded 4,583 men; those who protested tended to be men who feared needles. This sort of blanket collection of very personal evidence would be unlikely to go so smoothly in America, given Americans' focus on privacy rights. One man evaded the process by having a co-worker impersonate him; Britain's lack of uniform picture IDs facilitated the impersonation. Only when the co-worker told other co-workers, who then told police, did the police finally locate the man whose DNA matched what was left at the crime scenes.

The following account of the first American application of DNA evidence to a capital case synthesizes the following sources: the coverage of the case in the *Washington Post*, especially extensive feature stories by Dana Priest; articles about the trials in the *Richmond Times-Dispatch*; *Stalking Justice*, the 1995 book on the case by Paul Mones, which follows the perspective of detective Joseph Horgas; and a chapter in 1997's *Journey into Darkness* by John Douglas and Mark Olshaker (Douglas was the FBI agent who pioneered profiling).

On the night of January 22, 1984, in Arlington, Carolyn Hamm, an attorney who worked with architects, suffered a terrible death. Her attacker entered her home, where she lived alone, through a small basement window. The attacker violated her sexually, tied her hands behind her with the cord of her own venetian blinds, and hanged her by a noose made of rope taken from her own rolled-up carpet. The killer emptied her purse onto the floor and took her cash, but nothing else.

Within two weeks, Arlington police arrested thirty-seven-year-old David Vasquez. A mentally handicapped janitor, Vasquez lived with his mother in Manassas, which by the highways in 1984 was about an hour from Arlington. And Vasquez could not drive. He came to the attention of police because two neighbors of Hamm claimed to have seen him near Hamm's house. When police took him to the station for what started as routine questioning, he insisted that he was not in Arlington, but his alibi could not be confirmed. Then the detectives lied, which is legal: They told him that his fingerprints were in Hamm's home. They yelled at him. Vasquez gave in; over the next two days he offered three confessions to killing Hamm, each somewhat different. Douglas and Olshaker judge the confessions harshly:

> [Vasquez had] been interrogated in a method which was inappro-
> priate and which we [the FBI] would have known to be ineffective
> for someone of his passivity and lack of sophistication. Transcripts
> and interviews showed they'd used the good cop/bad cop technique
> on him, raising voices, slamming the table, and surrounding him in
> a small interrogation room with no windows and full of cigarette
> smoke. Eventually, he just seems to have broken down. His entire
> confession seems based on information they'd already given him.

Aside from the confession and the two witnesses, police had little to place Vasquez at the scene. A shoe print of his size was near
Hamm's home, and hair that shared some characteristics of his was
at the scene. By the twenty-first century, hair identification had been
discredited except for general features.

For the defense, Vasquez could offer his shaky alibi and evidence
that his blood type did not match the semen at the scene. This distinction would seem definitive, but police reasoned that Vasquez had
an accomplice. The judge disallowed the first two confessions, but
allowed the third because before giving it, Vasquez had finally been
properly Mirandized. Mones writes that the defense attorneys asked
for a plea deal, in part because they did not want to risk putting their
easily confused client on the witness stand in his own defense.

On February 4, 1985, Vasquez took an Alford plea to second-
degree murder and burglary, a significantly lesser charge that left off
the rape. Indeed, the plea may signal a lack of confidence on both
sides and raise questions if the case should ever have been scheduled
for trial. In an Alford plea, the defendant does not admit guilt but
recognizes that the evidence could lead to conviction of a greater
charge. The judge recommended "intense therapy" for Vasquez.
Instead, he went to Buckingham Correctional Center, a crowded
maximum-security prison that offered only sporadic counseling.
Vasquez, slight and passive, did not fare well at Buckingham. A convicted murderer doing his time at the prison told Dana Priest of the
Washington Post, "When he came to the system, the system failed to
properly classify him. Security personnel failed to properly protect
him, and the man suffered punishment most of us could not relate

to." Vasquez avoided getting into official trouble and eventually in 1987 earned an immense reward, a single cell.

In 1987, on September 19 and the night of October 2, both Fridays, two white professional women who lived (mostly) alone in Richmond were murdered by strangulation. The attacks occurred in their homes, with the killer entering by back windows. They had been raped and securely bound at the hands and neck. The noose was especially fiendish as it could be twisted and untwisted to choke the victim. Petechial hemorrhages, broken blood vessels in the eyes, revealed that the killer had repeatedly tortured the women by this method. The women showed no defensive wounds, suggesting that the killer subdued them quickly. The killer left significant amounts of semen at the scenes. The women were Debbie Dudley Davis, who worked in accounting at a local weekly newspaper, and Dr. Susan Hellams of the Medical College of Virginia. Davis was unmarried; Hellams's husband was away doing graduate work and discovered the body when he came home.

On November 22, 1987, fifteen-year-old Diane Cho endured a similar death at her family's apartment. The setting this time was nearby Chesterfield County. This attack was very bold: The killer entered her room, subdued her, and tormented her while her parents were in the next room. The closeness in time of the three attacks deserves mention. The local police linked the three cases based on the similar crime scenes.

In Arlington, five days later, at the start of the Thanksgiving holiday on November 27, Susan Tucker, a technical writer for the U.S. Forestry Service whose husband was in Wales, died in similar fashion. Neighbors asked police to check on her on December 1. The extent of the decomposition placed the death several days before, hence the November 27 dating. Detective Joseph Horgas entered the case as the primary investigator. As he surveyed the Tucker home and viewed her body, Horgas thought of Carolyn Hamm.

Horgas had been out of town when Hamm's body was discovered; thus the case went to other detectives. When he returned, Horgas did look at files about a series of break-ins and rapes at homes near Hamm's committed by a black man who wore a mask. When he offered these parallels to his superiors, they rebuffed him.

But now that he owned the Tucker case, he could explore these parallels anew, especially as Tucker's home was across a wooded hill from Hamm's residence. He listed the similarities between the two deaths: single white women, found nude, bound in similar fashion; rapes; methods of entry; lack of fingerprints; presence of semen. He visited David Vasquez in prison, accompanied by a defense attorney. Horgas asked if Vasquez would give the name of his accomplice; Vasquez protested his innocence. When they left the prison, Horgas bluntly told the attorney that Vasquez surely was innocent.

Then Horgas saw bulletins from Richmond about their cases. Horgas gained entrance to a task force meeting in Richmond and got to see the evidence. Convinced that all the killings were related, he returned to Arlington and did what he started to do in 1984: look at reports of rapes and burglaries in the vicinity from before the attack on Hamm. A relentless researcher, he found ten rapes and four other break-ins. He interviewed nine of the rape victims; one refused to speak with him. The specifics convinced Horgas that these were related crimes. Horgas developed the theory that the killer moved from burglary to rape to murder. The perpetrator perfected a method of entry through small windows. He chose victims and locations so that he could spend significant time torturing them. He used a similar series of commands, almost a prepared script, during the rapes. He often took cash, only cash, usually taken from the spilled-out contents of pocketbooks. The Richmond cases fit the pattern. Significantly, Horgas's decision was not based on gut reactions or instincts. He methodically developed his theory through charting the specifics of the crimes.

His analysis encountered resistance in three areas. First, his theory included a closed case, the Hamm case, and his Arlington coworkers resented his reexamination of their work. However, the current Commonwealth Attorney for Arlington County, Helen F. Fahey, was receptive to the theory. Next, the Richmond detectives would not accept that the same person did the killings in Richmond and Arlington. Lastly, the FBI profilers, who had consulted with Richmond police, were reluctant to accept that a black man would serially kill white women. In their studies of crimes they had never encountered the interracial dimension that was crucial to Horgas's theory. Indeed, at the time, the FBI professed no experience with a black serial killer, aside from the Atlanta child killings. This particular resistance is an interesting contrast to the racial mythology of the past that black men posed a threat to white women; this mythology had often served as the excuse for lynchings.

On December 29, 1987, FBI profilers visited Arlington to consult on the Tucker case. "Profiling" is the common term for the analysis conducted by the FBI's Behavioral Science Unit, devised by John Douglas, among others, in the 1970s. Using the specifics of the crime scene and the victim, profilers develop a cluster of the killer's probable traits. Profiling can seem mystical and even hopelessly general, unless accompanied by rational explanations for the theories. Profilers employ psychology, statistics on traits that often correlate, and, perhaps gruesomely, insights gained from interviews with convicts.

Once Horgas had the agents engaged in a vigorous question-and-answer session about Tucker, he gingerly introduced the Richmond cases, then Hamm. The agents probed more and eventually assented to his theory. They emphasized the elaborate and torturous binding of the victims as the killer's signature—the trait that marks the crimes as his. The bindings and the scripts from the rapes showed that the attacker sought control and mastery over his victims. Such desire for control appeared among solitary killers who did not bring accomplices. The profilers agreed with Horgas that the rapes showed how the killer practiced and perfected his methods; a killer would not suddenly commit an elaborate murder without preliminary crimes. The agents dismissed Vasquez as too simple-minded to be the organized, detail-attentive killer of the five women.

Just before the meeting with the FBI, Horgas delivered the biological evidence to the New York office of Lifecodes, a company that conducted DNA tests. Lifecodes already had samples from

Richmond; the police there wanted proof that the same man did all three killings. Horgas wanted Lifecodes to compare the samples from Hamm, Tucker, and several of the Arlington-area rapes (for which he had evidence) to each other and to the Richmond evidence.

Horgas lacked patience, so he filled time waiting for Lifecodes' reply by researching more files. The profilers had suggested that a criminal begins his crimes in an area familiar to him, so Horgas figured that the criminal lived near the scene of the first rape. Visiting the area reminded Horgas of a case there years ago of a black kid suspected of burglary and of setting a fire. In one of the early rapes, the attacker put the victim in the trunk of her car and set the backseat on fire; she escaped, or the first death would have been hers. Records showed that this man, now age twenty-five, had been arrested for burglary early in 1984, convicted, sent to prison, and then released to a halfway house in Richmond in 1987. The dates of his incarceration matched the gap of time between the killings of Hamm and Davis. The man had a mother and grandmother living in Arlington, close to the homes of Hamm and Tucker. Thus, on January 6, 1988, Timothy Spencer became the prime suspect.

The director of the halfway house confirmed for Horgas that Spencer had signed himself out on the weekend evenings of the Richmond deaths and had been allowed to go to Arlington for Thanksgiving. As in the past, Richmond police did not share Horgas's enthusiasm for this suspect; they could not overcome the idea that interracial sexual murder was unprecedented. They kept Spencer under surveillance and nearly arrested him when his female companions engaged in shoplifting. But after two weeks, Richmond wearied of the expense; unconvinced of Horgas's theory, they decided to curtail the surveillance.

Commonwealth Attorney Fahey proved herself to be Horgas's most powerful ally. She worried that the opportunity to catch Spencer would be lost and that he was a danger to society—given the short time frames of the attacks. So she let Horgas explain his theory and show his accumulated evidence to a grand jury. On January 20, the grand jury indicted Spencer for the burglary, rape, and murder of Susan Tucker. With the assistance of Richmond police, Horgas arrested Spencer that night outside the halfway house.

On the ride back to Arlington, detectives only told Spencer that his indictment was for burglary. But he was suspicious that seven police cars would be needed for a burglary arrest. He asked if he was suspected of a murder. He volunteered a blood sample. Once in Arlington, detectives brought up the deaths of Carolyn Hamm and Susan Tucker. Through hours of interrogation, Spencer maintained his innocence.

An evidence technician eventually matched a fragment of glass found in Spencer's camouflage coat to the type of glass from Tucker's broken window. This tenuous link was not what Horgas wanted. He received what he wanted on March 16. Lifecodes reported that Spencer's DNA matched that from the Arlington-area rapes, from Tucker, and from Davis and Hellams in Richmond. The Hamm sample was too degraded to test. Horgas relished the vindication of his research.

Virginia schedules trials quickly. The trial for Susan Tucker's death occurred in July 1988, not quite six months after the arrest. The prosecution's case consisted principally of the DNA tests, so Fahey relied on geneticists to educate the jurors about the technology. The defense attorneys, though prodded by the judge, offered no experts to refute the DNA evidence. They admitted that Spencer was in Arlington for Thanksgiving, but argued that he was almost wholly in the company of family during the weekend. Spencer took the stand and denied his involvement. Contrary to what prosecutors do on TV shows, Fahey declined to cross-examine him. She let her case stand on the science, which she told the jury was completely conclusive. The jury convicted after five hours of deliberation. The same jury recommended execution.

The defense attorneys may have been reluctant to question the DNA evidence because they had confirmed it. Cellmark, a rival of Lifecodes, had analyzed samples for them and rendered a judgment similar to that from Lifecodes. Unable to refute the DNA, the defense attorneys tried to ignore it.

The remaining trials continued like falling dominos. In September 1988, Spencer was convicted for killing Debbie Davis. In January 1989, he was convicted in the death of Susan Hellams. In the May 1989 trial for the slaying of Diane Cho, the prosecutors could not rely on DNA as the sample had been degraded at the scene. So they used evidence of the other offenses, "signature crimes," to show that Cho was part of a precisely definable series of attacks. The prosecutors also submitted that the three Richmond victims frequented a local mall; while under surveillance, Spencer lingered at this mall. Spencer was convicted again. Among the prosecutors for this case was Warren Von Schuch, who would later prosecute Beverly Monroe (see page 106). Jeffrey L. Everhart led the defenses in the Richmond trials; unlike the Arlington attorneys, he attacked the DNA evidence. In an opening statement, he argued, "It is not ready to stand the test of convicting a person of the crimes of murder, rape, and burglary." In summation he attacked the geneticist from the company that did the testing as giving "a sales pitch, worthy of any used car salesman in the nation, from the witness stand. . . They make money from doing this testing. This DNA testing is not ready to hurdle the mountain."

In each trial, the juries also voted for execution, and the judges so sentenced Spencer. Fahey said that given this record of convictions and death sentences, that she would not try him for Hamm's death nor for the rapes.

Horgas never forgot Vasquez, and he relentlessly urged Fahey to seek his release. But the DNA analysis was inconclusive due to the degraded sample, so it did not absolutely clear Vasquez. Horgas even sent samples to a company in California that tried to replicate the DNA for analysis, but their procedures failed in this instance. To bolster their position, Horgas and Fahey appealed to the FBI. John Douglas personally joined a team to reanalyze the evidence from Hamm and Tucker. Douglas signed the report that concluded that the same man had done both deeds. Fahey forwarded this report to Gov. Gerald Baliles in October 1988. After a review by the Board of Parole and Pardons, Governor Baliles issued a pardon to Vasquez. He left prison on January 4, 1989, and returned to live with his mother in Manassas. Eventually, the Virginia legislature granted Vasquez $117,000, to be given in monthly payments, thus assuring him an income.

Spencer's appeals centered on the admissibility of DNA evidence and on the handling of his samples. During a sentencing hearing, Spencer complained about the "lowlife" DNA experts and accused Horgas of faking the evidence against him. He also, while in court, gave Horgas the finger. The legal documents were not so accusatory, but they did try to question the methods of Lifecodes. Federal courts upheld the right of state courts to admit the DNA evidence.

Spencer died by electrocution late on the night of April 27, 1994. Specifically he died for killing Davis, as the appeals in that case were exhausted first. Spencer always proclaimed his innocence. The execution had other notable features, aside from being the first that resulted from DNA evidence. The prison system's head doctor refused to take part to pronounce Spencer dead due to new American Medical Association guidelines that declared participation in executions violated medical ethics. A new law allowed a victim's family members to attend executions, but no family members wanted to watch Spencer die.

The Richmond slayings form the basis of *Postmortem* (1990), Patricia Cornwell's first novel. Cornwell's recurring character, Dr. Kay Scarpetta, the Chief Medical Examiner of the Commonwealth of Virginia, goes beyond her lab to immerse herself in the investigation of a series of attacks against professional women. The other main characters are a rumpled police detective and an FBI profiler. Like most fiction writers, Cornwell uses only the most basic aspects of the real case, and then spins events in her own direction. The novel's villain shares few traits with Timothy Spencer, and Cornwell artfully shifts the racial aspects. But the torture and methods of death are gruesomely close to the reality. The novel does not emphasize DNA, though later books in the Scarpetta series do.

Postmortem and the series present Scarpetta as an advocate of up-to-date technology; the novels make Virginia look progressive for embracing this technology. Cornwell had worked in the Medical Examiner's Office as a computer analyst, and so she wrote with technical awareness. Through the 1990s, her novels educated readers on how crime fighting had become scientific. In the early novels, Dr. Scarpetta seems out of place: a woman from outside Virginia surrounded by Southern men who are suspicious of a woman entering the male fields of government and crime-fighting. Scarpetta has a real-life counterpart. Coming from New York to the Medical Examiner's Office in the 1970s, Dr. Marcella Fierro rose through the ranks to become Virginia's Chief Medical Examiner in 1994. Cornwell dedicated her fourth novel to Dr. Fierro, with the line, "You taught Scarpetta well." Dr. Fierro will appear in a later chapter of this book.

CHAPTER 6

The Case of Elizabeth Haysom and Jens Soering, 1985–90

Derek Haysom lay supine in the massive spray of his own blood. Two long gashes crossed his face. A deep cut in his neck had severed his major blood vessels and accounted for the volume of blood. His body exhibited other knife wounds: eleven cuts on his chest, fourteen on his back, and slices across his palms that suggested that he had actually grabbed at the weapon. His wife Nancy also suffered a gaping cut across her throat, along with stab wounds to her chest and side, among other less lethal strikes.

The Haysoms died in their home, which showed no forced entry and no indications of robbery. Derek lay near the door in the main room, Nancy in the kitchen. The dining area, encrusted with dried blood, included a table with one place set for eating, with a plate of food, a bowl, and a glass. Three chairs had been pushed back from the table. On first glance, police recognized the incongruity: that the bloody, ferocious attack interrupted a civilized-looking meal. The third party at that meal, whoever he or she was, would know what happened, and might even be the killer. The killer, an accomplice, or someone else had swirled the blood about while wearing socks, probably to obliterate shoeprints. These swirls led to lurid early speculation that the killer(s) had "danced in the blood"—a common phrase in original reports.

The Haysoms had fancifully named the house Loose Chippings, an obscure literary reference according to Nancy. The location was Boonsboro in Bedford County, near Lynchburg. The Haysoms, regular church members, had not attended Palm Sunday services nor the bridge games that they frequented. Concerned about these absences and alarmed by a call from the Haysoms' daughter that she could not reach her parents, a neighbor with a key went with friends to check at the house. They left upon seeing the carnage and summoned the police. Due to the Haysoms' absence from church, police set the death date as Saturday evening, March 30, 1985.

Over a year later, on April 30, 1986, police in London questioned Elizabeth Haysom, the daughter who had called about not being able to reach her parents, and her boyfriend Jens Soering about a check-cashing scam. Evidence at the couple's lodgings made the police suspicious about their pasts. In about five more weeks, Elizabeth and Jens confessed to involvement in the deaths of Elizabeth's parents, or more accurately, they told stories that admitted their involvement. These stories shifted as time passed. The early versions placed sole blame on Jens as the killer. Jens would eventually change his version to claim that Elizabeth committed the crime alone. The couple had gone to Washington, D.C., on that weekend, and some evidence suggests that one of them stayed there and the other went to the Haysom home. Which one? Or is it possible that both went to Boonsboro that night?

The case draws attention for its horrible irony: that two honors students from privileged backgrounds could be involved in such a gruesome murder of parents. The evidence in this case is also puzzling. Is it possible to determine definitively what occurred? The preserved letters of Elizabeth and Jens from before the attack discuss killing her parents. After their arrests in London, they both admitted being involved. This much everyone accepts. But since Elizabeth and Jens blame each other for doing the actual killings, does evidence exist to determine which one (or both?) was at Loose Chippings that night?

The following account relies on the reporting in the *Washington Post*, Charlottesville's newspaper *The Daily Progress*, and the *Roanoke Times and World-News*, and on retrospective journalism in other Virginia news sources. The following also makes use of the 1990 book on the case *Beyond Reason* by Ken Englade, which is both valuable and problematic, as we shall see.

At ages seventy-two and fifty-three respectively, Derek and Nancy Haysom had led eventful lives. Born in South Africa, Derek served in the British military in World War II. An engineer by training, Derek entered management and oversaw a steel mill in Rhodesia. As that country, led by Ian Smith, sought to break away from Great Britain and establish white minority rule, Derek continued to be racially neutral in hiring and promotions at the mill. His policies led to his house arrest. The Haysoms fled the country, first to Luxembourg, where Derek managed a chocolate company, and then to Canada, where Derek became a steel mill executive.

Nancy was Derek's second wife. His first he had wed in South Africa, but she left him and their three children. Nancy was American, the daughter of a geologist who eventually settled his family in South Africa where he worked for a mining operation. Nancy too had a previous spouse and two children when she met Derek. Derek adopted Nancy's children. Elizabeth was their only child together. Very little information exists about the Haysoms' first marriages. When Derek finally retired from his series of jobs in 1982, they settled near Lynchburg, where Nancy had grown up. Nancy's mother's family was prominent in Lynchburg and included, as a distant cousin, Lady Astor, the first woman elected to Britain's House of Commons. In fact, Lady Astor was Nancy's godmother.

Elizabeth and Jens met in the fall of 1984 as first-year students in the Echols Scholar Program on the Grounds of the University of

Virginia. (UVA Cavaliers do not use the word "campus.") UVA values its its power to attract outstanding high school students. One such draw is the Echols Scholar Program: In their first year, Echols students live together, receive attention from their own dean, and enjoy freedom to design their own academic programs. The Jefferson Scholars, who numbered only eighteen that year, receive huge academic scholarships. Both Elizabeth and Jens were in the Echols Program; Jens was a prestigious Jefferson Scholar.

Elizabeth stood apart from her fellow scholars for her striking accent, an amalgam of English, South African, and Canadian inflections; for her sophisticated international background; and for her age, twenty years old. The Haysoms had sent her to private schools, and she spent her high school years in England at Wycombe Abbey, a boarding school, where she stayed an extra year. The public version is that her final year's courses did not earn good enough grades for the ambitious Elizabeth to get into Cambridge, so she stayed for another year. After the end of exams that extra year, she and a close girlfriend ran away, disappearing from July through October, when they went to the British consulate in Germany. They told stories of working subsistence jobs across Europe and meeting other youthful travelers, some of them dangerous. The chief source for this episode is a letter to Nancy from a British officer whom the Haysoms implored to monitor reports in case Elizabeth appeared. This officer judged the girls to be in desperate, forlorn states when they went to the consulate, though they only wanted passage back to England. The officer shepherded them for eight days, eventually getting them back to London. The Haysoms brought Elizabeth back to Boonsboro, and through the spring the family planned on sending Elizabeth to the University of Virginia in the fall.

Both Elizabeth and Jens seemed aloof among their Echols Scholar peers. Probably their international backgrounds drew them together. Jens was the son of a West German diplomat and had grown up in Atlanta, though he had lived in Thailand, Cyprus, and Germany. The romance developed through their first semester. By December, they shared fantasies, including letters in which Elizabeth fantasized about the deaths of her parents.

Elizabeth's animus against her parents defies explanation. Her half brother Howard Haysom (Nancy's son), a Houston physician, claims that Derek and Nancy wanted to split up Elizabeth and Jens, though why remains obscure; how frequently the Haysoms even met Jens is uncertain. Years later, Jens would explain the enmity by referencing "the photographs": Police found in Nancy's art studio five photographs of Elizabeth nude in profile. Jens later said that Elizabeth showed him these pictures without comment; Jens suggested that the pictures implied sexual abuse. Yet Elizabeth never specified her complaints. Regarding the pictures, in one later interview with police Elizabeth claimed that Nancy took the pictures to humiliate her, but then Elizabeth denied in court that her parents abused her. Then she claimed that Nancy slept with her. . . As we shall see, Elizabeth told many things.

After the killings, the Bedford County Sheriff assigned the case to thirty-year-old investigator Ricky Gardner. On April 8, 1985, he interviewed Elizabeth in the company of another detective. Gardner audiotaped all his interviews. In these interviews, Elizabeth explained that she had spent the weekend that her parents died in Washington with Jens. She went on odd tangents; Gardner found her difficult to talk to and felt put off by her rather calm manner under the circumstances. Elizabeth later complained that Gardner was hostile to her. Gardner was suspicious and made an investigative act that would prove significant: He checked the odometer reading on the agency's receipt for the rental car that Elizabeth and Jens took to Washington. It read 669 miles. From Charlottesville to Washington is about 120 miles; from Charlottesville to Boonsboro is about 80 miles. He realized that the car could have gone to Washington, then to Boonsboro, then back to Washington, then to Charlottesville, given the recorded mileage.

Amorphous suspicions are not evidence, and Gardner had no other reasons to pursue Elizabeth as a suspect. She and Jens went to Europe in the summer and settled into a rental house for their second year at UVA. That fall, Gardner sought a formal interview with Jens; he wanted to confirm Elizabeth's account of the weekend and to get finger- and footprints from Jens. Most family members and associates of the Haysoms had given prints, but Jens kept putting off the date. On October 12, 1985, he left America. Elizabeth followed him the next day.

London police detained them on April 30, 1986, and took them in for questioning about suspicious behavior at the Spencer & Marks department store. A store detective watched them enter together, ignore each other in the store, get cash refunds for goods they brought into the store, make purchases with checks, and come back together outside. The detective alerted police, who brought Elizabeth and Jens to the station, where they let police see checkbooks, blanks because they had been newly issued, which featured lots of purchases at Spencer & Marks. Detectives asked for permission to search their lodgings. Elizabeth first said no, but Jens agreed. At the flat, police found a collection of thirty-two Spencer & Marks bags filled with merchandise, each with a card detailing which store the purchases had come from and what they had been wearing on the shopping trip. Their scam involved using fake names to open bank accounts, using the new checks to make purchases, returning the purchases for cash, then repeating the process at another branch of the store.

Police also found a cache of documents, including diary entries that detailed another scam to get money: reporting travelers checks as lost and getting the cash advance. Elizabeth and Jens pulled this ruse during their travels; they had been to Asia, Russia, and other places in Europe. Police also found letters that discussed murdering parents and, amazingly, that mentioned Detective Gardner. As the British authorities prepared the check fraud charges, the detectives tried to figure out whom to call about a possible murder.

Elizabeth and Jens broke several "commandments of crime." One commandment is not to put criminal enterprises onto paper; the diary they kept explains a series of scams while they traveled. Another commandment is not to save incriminating stuff; for whatever reason, perhaps sentimental value, Elizabeth and Jens saved the early letters about killing the Haysoms. Another commandment is to make police get search warrants, instead of being agreeable and allowing police to see incriminating stuff. The London police later wondered if they could have gotten a judge to sign a warrant to

search the flat. Elizabeth and Jens later broke another commandment of crime: make police work for evidence rather than confess
too easily. Had they followed these commandments, Elizabeth and
Jens might have escaped.

The London police invited Gardner and Commonwealth Attorney James Updike to be present when Elizabeth and Jens were interrogated about the letters. By usual practice, London police taped
most of their conversations with suspects. In early June, before
shifting teams of officials from London and Bedford County, Jens
and Elizabeth each confessed to involvement in the murders.

The basic elements of their separate stories are as follows: They
went to Washington that weekend; she stayed behind to do things to
establish an alibi; he drove to Loose Chippings; a talk between Jens
and the Haysoms at the table while Jens was eating turned into a
violent argument that resulted in the deaths; Jens disposed of the
knife and bloody clothes as he drove back to Washington. The detail
about the meal raises questions about state of mind, about whether
murder was the original intent or if the deaths resulted from a quar-
rel. But this possibility, which suggests manslaughter rather than
intentional murder, never got much consideration from authorities—probably because of the letters.

Beyond this basic outline, specifics were elusive and changing.
What Elizabeth and Jens did in Washington shifted according to
who told the story when. Variously, Elizabeth claimed that according to plan she saw several films, buying two tickets each time to
establish an alibi; another time she claimed to have decided to buy
the tickets on her own; another time that she saw only one movie.
The *Norfolk Virginian-Pilot* helpfully pointed out five shifting statements from Elizabeth about the murder weapon: She and Jens
bought a martial arts knife as a present for Jens's brother; they
bought the knife as the murder weapon; Jens bought the knife himself; they did not buy a knife; they bought a knife but Jens used a
steak knife on the Haysoms.

Investigators heard dramatic tales from Elizabeth. She claimed
that she had been raped as a young child at her Swiss boarding
school, that she had been punched at her Canadian school by

roughnecks as a threat to her father, who was quarreling with a workers union, and that Nancy's first husband bit pieces of flesh from his infant child. Family members could not verify these tales. Elizabeth may have told the truth; she may have exaggerated; she may have fabricated. What to believe from Elizabeth was always an open question.

Elizabeth agreed to return to America. After serving time in England for the fraud charges, she waived extradition in May 1987. In Virginia, her court-appointed attorneys Hugh Jones and Andrew Davis negotiated a plea in which she pled guilty to accessory to murder before-the-fact. The sentence would be same as for first-degree murder, but the lawyers stressed the vital distinction: Her plea meant that she was not at the scene of the crime.

Elizabeth still had to endure a sentencing hearing before Judge William Sweeney, at which her attorneys would try to convince the judge to be merciful. The hearing began in August 1987, recessed, and resumed for the defense presentation in October. The defense offered a psychiatrist; character witnesses, including a Narcotics Anonymous counselor from England who had helped Elizabeth while she was in prison; and Elizabeth herself. She told a version of events in which she did not participate in the actual killings, nor even in the planning. She wanted her parents out of her life, but not murdered—her distinction. She had complained about them to Jens and fantasized about their demise. That weekend in Washington, discussion about the Haysoms enraged Jens, and he went to Boonsboro to confront them. She let him go, aware that he might become violent with them; she wanted to be alone so that she could score drugs. She claimed to have been in the throes of drug dependency. When Jens returned, she was shocked at what he had done. She stayed with him out of love. She pled guilty because she regretted her inflammatory letters to Jens and because in Washington she had let him become angry and did not stop him from leaving. This version placed maximum responsibility for planning and execution on Jens, with her supplying the ill-defined motivation. Prosecutor Updike hammered her on cross-examination about her previous tales and about her intentions towards her parents. She admitted to a string of lies, but held to this version. On October 8, 1987, Judge Sweeney sentenced her to ninety years in prison, forty-five for each death.

The hearing ended in frustration for Howard Haysom, who had convinced himself that Elizabeth was in the house at the time of the killings. He recalled his mother mentioning that Elizabeth and Jens would visit that weekend—though Elizabeth had visited the previous weekend, and perhaps Howard confused the dates. Howard was sure that his parents would not admit Jens without Elizabeth. Updike knew of Howard's strong suspicions.

Yet by not fighting extradition and then by pleading guilty, Elizabeth had her version—in its broad outline—accepted as the official version. And it did match, mostly, what Jens was saying in England. For three years, this version held sway, until Jens changed his story.

In 1990, St, Martin's published *Beyond Reason* by Ken Englade. Though the book presents Elizabeth as wily and manipulative, Englade accepts her version that Jens killed the Haysoms. He opens with a fictionalized scene, including dialogue, of the Haysoms working in their garden on March 30, 1985. That evening, they hear a persistent knocking at their door. They answer it to see a young man with thick glasses and a five-foot-eight build (just like Jens). Derek wonders why Elizabeth is not with him, but Nancy invites him in and offers a plate of food. By presenting as a fact in the opening chapter that Jens went to Loose Chippings that night, the book makes definitive what continued to be a matter of debate. If Englade and his publisher had waited, the book could have recorded the case's next phase.

In 1990, Jens went on trial for murder in Virginia. Jens had fought extradition. In Great Britain, his lawyers argued that he should not be returned to Virginia because he could face a possible death sentence if convicted. (Among Western democracies, the United States is alone in allowing capital punishment, and in this and other cases America's allies have hesitated to extradite fugitives.) Judges and, in 1988, the House of Lords denied his appeals. Richard Neaton, a Detroit attorney hired by Jens's father, arranged to have the matter taken to the European Commission on Human Rights, which referred the matter to the Court of Human Rights. At these proceedings, West Germany offered to try Jens, who was a

German citizen. On July 7, 1989, by a 19-0 vote, the court refused to allow the extradition. The court did not baldly claim that the existence of capital punishment in Virginia was the reason, but referred to the conditions for prisoners under death sentence:

> The manner in which it [capital punishment] is imposed or executed, the personal circumstances of the condemned person and a disproportionality to the gravity of the crime committed, as well as the conditions of detention awaiting execution, are examples of factors capable of bringing the treatment or punishment received by the condemned person within the proscription under Article 3 [which forbids degrading punishment].

In early August 1989, Updike relented: Jens would be charged with first-degree murder, not capital murder. Britain then sent him to Virginia.

Prosecutors possessed a sequence of incriminating statements from Jens. At trial, they relied on taped statements in London in which he said that he did drive to see the Haysoms and that an argument ensued; a statement from June 8, 1986, given to Gardner and to British police; and a statement from December 30, 1986, given to West German officials as part of Jens's efforts before the European Court to be sent to Germany for trial. On June 8, Jens refused to be taped, but Gardner took notes. The December 30 confession had been taped and then translated from German; it largely matched details in Gardner's notes from June. Jens repudiated these statements, claiming that he took responsibility expecting that as a diplomat's son and as a youthful offender, that he would be sent to Germany, where he would get a sentence of about ten years; by taking responsibility, he sought that Elizabeth would not face the death penalty for what she did.

In Jens's new story, while they were in Washington, Elizabeth left him for a foray supposedly related to drugs, and he bought the film tickets to establish her alibi. She shocked him by telling him at her return that she had killed her parents. To bolster this story, the defense presented the film tickets and hotel receipts: Soering's father claimed to have found them among his son's possessions late in 1985 while cleaning out Jens's Charlottesville room. Strikingly, police had to admit that they had not searched Jens's room. The alibi story included that a meal from room service was ordered for the hotel room, which the hotel bill verified. The prosecution would later argue that these documents established only that either Jens or Elizabeth stayed in Washington, but did not establish which one.

To fight this new defense, the prosecution had in its arsenal Jens's confessions and Elizabeth, who testified against Jens at trial. But the cross-accusations between Jens and Elizabeth necessitated that the Commonwealth answer this question: What physical and circumstantial evidence establishes Jens (not Elizabeth) as the killer? Put another way, what evidence would convince the jury to trust the original version rather than Jens's new version? Could Jens be placed at Loose Chippings on that night?

The Commonwealth offered the following. At the funeral for the Haysoms, attendees noticed bruises on Jens's face and a bandage on his left hand; these injuries matched his original confession. His blood type matched that found at the scene, but he had a common type. And a sock print in the blood matched his foot size. This last piece became the most contentious. The swirling of blood at the scene had defeated most shoeprint analysis, except for in a few places. Updike produced a state expert who, with the aid of transparencies, matched Jens's foot size to a bloody sock print. Richard Neaton, Jens's attorney, argued on cross-examination and at summation that Elizabeth's foot size also matched.

Jurors later admitted that deliberations began with a 6-6 vote and that the sock print was significant in their decision. At least one juror claimed that it was the most convincing piece of evidence against Jens. The jury discussed for four hours, then returned two verdicts of guilty. Jens received two life sentences.

In the mid-1990s, Gail Sterling Marshall took over Jens's appeals. A former deputy attorney general, she stressed the failure of Neaton to refute the sock print evidence, noting that experts to refute the match were available at trial. She continued that after the case, Neaton had his license suspended in Michigan: In 1993

Neaton admitted to being "impaired by an emotional or mental disability" from 1989 through 1992. Marshall also expressed doubt about Judge Sweeney's impartiality, as he had said in a magazine interview that he figured that Elizabeth did the planning while Jens carried out the plans. And Sweeney knew Derek and Nancy. Further, Marshall pointed out that a bloody slashing murder had been committed by two vagrants six days after the Haysoms' deaths; she suggested that Elizabeth had met these men and got them to kill her parents. The federal court rejected all the claims, and in 2001 Marshall exhausted Jens's appeals. (The blood evidence was destroyed or degraded, so DNA analysis could not be performed.)

In the new century, Jens and Marshall turned their efforts to seeking parole. He continued to maintain his absolute innocence, a difficult stand as parole boards usually want to hear remorse. Jens offered a measure of remorse in a 2006 letter to Parole Board Chair Helen F. Fahey, who had earlier in her career prosecuted Timothy Spencer. Returning to the infamous nude photos that Nancy took of Elizabeth, Jens wrote that when Elizabeth showed them to him and said nothing, he let the moment pass. Had he pursued the matter, gotten her to talk, convinced her to go for counseling at UVA, and gone with her to counseling, perhaps she would have begun to resolve her enmity with her parents, and perhaps then she would not have killed them. He wrote that he wished that he could have been more sensitive to Elizabeth at that time.

In prison, Jens turned to religion; many prisoners do, but few have Jens's literary skill to express their conversion to the outside world. He devoted himself to "centering prayer," a technique involving repetition of a single word as a means to enter an uncluttered mental state where one can experience the spiritual. (Jens recommended the technique to Helen Fahey in his letter.) Uniting his religious interest with prison advocacy, he has authored letters or columns in national Catholic magazines, including *America*, *Christian Century*, and the *National Catholic Reporter*. Lucid and well-researched, the pieces mix his personal experiences with statistics, studies, and quotations from experts and politicians. He offers an insider's view of the impact of crime-fighting legislation: He claims that putting teenage offenders in adult prisons almost inevitably leads to sexual assault, not to the offenders being scared straight, and claims that major supporters for anti-parole reforms are prison contractors such as food service companies or prison healthcare providers. He wrote a striking essay on the suicide of his cellmate for *America*:

> What little I did come to know of Keith in our year together I liked a lot. He took a shower every day; he always used headphones while watching his 5-inch TV; he did not steal from me; he did not try to rape me or start a consensual sexual relationship with me; he did not use drugs or brew alcohol . . . he did not press conversation on me when I did not want it—which I never do. All this made Keith an ideal cellmate for me, a veritable gift from heaven. For all practical purposes, he was invisible, unnoticeable, absent.

Jens continues that he was moved by the irony that he, a Christian prison advocate, may have overlooked the needs of the man physically closest to him. Small religious presses published four books by Jens about prayer, prison reform, and the example of Jesus. Only the first book addresses, briefly, his version of his case. In 2004, as a sign of his high regard in the eyes of the Catholic Church, Jens received communion from the hands of Richmond's retired Bishop Walter Sullivan.

While Jens welcomes interviewers and through the years has been profiled by the press (and even has his own website, maintained by supporters), Elizabeth has refused to speak about the past. But she has not been silent. From 2003 through January 2008, she wrote eighty-nine columns for the *Fluvanna Review*, the local newspaper in the region where she is imprisoned. Given the title *Glimpses from Inside*, her pieces, for which she received no pay, offer very precise portraits of prison life and then draw small lessons. Whereas Jens seems to want his readers to be disturbed by the conditions and statistics that he offers, Elizabeth adopts a gentler tone. Environment probably accounts for much of the difference: He was in several tough prisons, while she lives in the honors unit of a women's facility. She describes how a group planned a performance of a Shakespeare play only to have it canceled, yet the group overcame disappointment and kept meeting. She describes amusingly how she and her cellmate rescued a bar of soap, an important commodity, which had fallen into their toilet. She describes how she adjusted to the special code of prison manners, such as not holding doors. Regarding the prisoners' service project to train dogs for eventual adoption, she writes of the dogs' citizenship or obedience tests, "As I watched (with absurd pride, nervousness, tension, and joy!) the dogs go through their tests (Dizzy's 'down' was spectacular!), it occurred to me that we inmates might benefit from a similar rigorous test of our good citizenship." Regarding prison industry—she does drafting; others repair eyeglasses or make furniture—she writes, "For some of us, being able to contribute towards the needs of others is a major step in reclaiming our humanity."

The publisher, Eric Allen, explained at the onset of the series, "We hope it brings awareness, promotes volunteerism at the prison, and deters crime . . . We're not glorifying her life. Her life is pretty dismal." But two other columnists resigned in protest, one stating, "I just think it's terribly inappropriate to be carrying firsthand writing by someone who had her parents murdered." Elizabeth herself eventually discontinued the columns.

The largely infraction-free prison lives of Elizabeth and Jens, along with their writings, bring up questions of recompense and rehabilitation. Such questions overshadowed the change in Virginia's governorship in January 2010. On January 12, outgoing governor Timothy Kaine wrote to the U.S. Department of Justice to approve Jens's transfer to a German prison, where Jens would serve at least two more years. Gail Marshall, who had stayed with the case, expressed relief. She had tried for the transfer earlier, but Kaine insisted on some prison time in Germany, to which the Germans had just recently agreed, according to Kaine. Upon taking office, new governor Robert McDonnell wrote to the Department of Justice to rescind the transfer. Both houses of the legislature unanimously passed a resolution decrying the proposed transfer. The Justice Department announced in March that it was reviewing whether a consent agreement could be revoked by a succeeding official. In early July, U.S. Attorney General Eric Holder wrote that he would honor Governor McDonnell's request: "Jens Soering will not be considered for transfer to Germany unless and until the Commonwealth of Virginia provides clear and unambiguous consent to such a transfer." Regarding the countermanding of a governor's consent by his successor, Holder declared this to be a matter for Virginia's courts, not his office. The following month, August 2010, Soering learned that he had been denied parole for the sixth time.

Amid this tumult, Jens's good service in prison meant little; one wonders if the legislators even knew about it. Aside from political posturing, at least three factors may work against Jens. First is the bloody brutality of the Haysoms' deaths; a member of the House of Delegates described the crime in a speech from the floor. Next is Jens's refusal to admit guilt—such is his right, yet it allows him to be cast as an unrepentant killer who has never accepted responsibility for his actions. Next is the perception that Europeans are less tough on crime than Americans and that Jens sought to evade American justice and continues this quest by trying to be transferred to Germany.

One of Elizabeth's final *Glimpses from Inside* columns describes a playful dog named Bonnie, whom the inmates are training but who has not been adopted because she looks to be part pit bull, though Elizabeth thinks she looks like a terrier. Elizabeth closes with this reflection: "For all I know, Bonnie is part pit. But she is also part lots of other dogs. We too are made of many parts and our most visible part, our crime, may not be the true determining factor as to whether we are violent, dangerous, predatory. Nonetheless, like Bonnie, it's a label that keeps us from going home."

CHAPTER 7

The Killing of John Kowalczyk, 1993–95

At about 7:45 P.M. on Thursday, June 10, 1993, thirty-eight-year-old John Kowalczyk and his twelve-year-old son Nicholas arrived at the parking lot of the office building at 115 Park Street SE in Vienna. They had spent several hours together as part of John's court-mandated visitation, and they were to meet John's ex-wife, Katherine, at this location. Nicholas told police that he left his father's truck to throw away trash from a fast-food meal, then heard a shot. His father had suffered a fatal gunshot to the front center of his skull. When Katherine arrived, they flagged down cars on Park Street to get someone to use a mobile phone to call for help. (Ironically, John often had one in his truck, according to friends.) Later that night, a police officer's notes recorded this cryptic statement from Nicholas: "They did not have to kill him, they only had to put him in jail for not paying child support."

James Zumwalt said this of the dead man: "The guy was a sleaze, an immoral individual. This guy got up every day of his life and said, 'Who can I screw over today?' Unfortunately, I was at the top of his list." A victim with such a list would provide the police with plenty of suspects.

The case regarding John Kowalczyk's death opened like a classical-style mystery novel with a group of suspects who had bad histories with the victim. Then the case became more hard-boiled, as it shifted into the milieu of people who operated on the fringes of the law and had criminal records and seemed mysteriously threatening. When the case came to trial, the issues concerned evidence and definitions: how to define and prove a criminal conspiracy; what evidence is necessary to prove that a conspiracy developed into action; and what evidence separates a conspirator from a murderer. The jury demanded very fine distinctions to be made, and the case offers a sobering primer for what trial lawyers must accomplish in court.

Amazingly, no book exists on this lively and complex case. The following narrative relies on the coverage of the events in the *Washington Post*. Patricia Davis stayed with the case, writing some of the articles during the investigation and covering the trial day-to-day.

The facts of his life suggest that John Kowalczyk was a man of great ambition and great achievement. He represents the immigrant dream: Born in a farmhouse in Poland in 1954, he eventually oversaw a self-started business involving millions of dollars worth of real estate. When he was eight, his parents settled in Yonkers, New York. According to his 1979 wedding announcement in the *Post*, he and Katherine were well-educated and well-placed. He had an M.A. from Georgetown University and worked for the Department of Defense. She was pursuing an M.A. at Catholic University and was employed at the Library of Congress. They eventually had two sons. In 1986, John left the government so that he and Katherine could form Jonathan Corp., a building and real estate company. They developed homes in Oakton to accommodate the mushrooming housing market in northern Virginia; they acquired tracts in Vienna and Oakton for future development; and they invested in commercial properties, one of which was at 115 Park Street, where John would die.

However, John and Katherine could not stay together. John began a relationship with Lisa Zumwalt; they had met in a real estate class in 1987. Three months after John's death, Lisa sought to refute the villainous portrayal of him by others: "John was a remarkable, special man. I was fortunate enough to have known him both in a business capacity as well as on a personal level. He was a devoted father, and a loving son and brother. He was a good friend to my children, and they loved him." Throughout the two years of the case, Lisa consistently defended John's character. His sister and parents showed their respect by attending the court proceedings, but unlike Lisa they would not speak to the press.

At the time of his death on June 10, 1993, John Kowalczyk was juggling several important matters. He was close, according to his bank, to resolving severe financial troubles. On the next day, June 11, John and Katherine were to attend a hearing regarding visitation matters concerning their younger son, who refused to see John. The ex-spouses faced a full custody trial in the fall. And on July 10, John planned to marry Lisa Zumwalt. As his death prevented all of these things from occurring, people who wanted them not to occur became suspects.

The first set of suspects involved finances. Kowalczyk had developed a reputation as an abrasive and demanding businessman. He willingly took disputes into court. Yet as development in northern Virginia spread to his Vienna properties, he thrived. One colleague referred to him as a "dynamo"; another dismissed him as a "lying snake." When the recession of the early 1990s stalled home building and hurt the value of commercial real estate, such as the property at 115 Park Street, several Jonathan Corp. projects went bankrupt. That John and Katherine still owned the company jointly even though they had become estranged complicated matters. Yet the company still held lots in a valuable housing development, and bank lawyers hoped that sale of those lots would retire the debt, which was about $700,000. One lawyer told the *Post*: "The irony of it all [the shooting], from the bank's perspective, was that he was very close to having the situation worked out."

Police probing these business problems wondered if Kowalczyk's history of tempestuous negotiations played any role in his death. One man attracted significant attention: Michael Highman, Katherine's brother. Michael and John had quarreled over a $300,000 commission for the sale of a property in Centreville; John won. Michael had also witnessed scenes involving John, Katherine, and the sons' resistance to having visits with John.

The other area for investigation concerned Kowalczyk's personal life. Starting in 1987, he formed a close bond with Lisa Zumwalt, wife of James Zumwalt. Though Lisa and John claimed at John's divorce proceedings that they had not been intimate, their spouses were convinced of an affair. As his relations with Katherine became more angry, Kowalczyk became more attentive to Lisa and her two children.

As the line quoted at the beginning of this chapter attests, James Zumwalt openly despised John Kowalczyk, and Kowalczyk's death did not diminish James's feelings. A lawyer, age forty-four at the time of the shooting, Zumwalt came from a prominent family. His father was Admiral Elmo Zumwalt, the chief of naval operations during the Vietnam War. Sadly, attached to Admiral Zumwalt's biography is the fact that he approved use of the toxic defoliant Agent Orange. James Zumwalt had served in Vietnam and in Desert Storm. Though he and Lisa divorced in 1989, he remained protective of her and their two children.

In April 1992, Zumwalt hired two private detectives: one to trail Kowalczyk and another, a comely young woman, to pretend to be an agent interested in a property deal and to seduce him. The first detective duly reported that Kowalczyk "acted like a dog after a bitch in heat" toward a woman at a hotel bar in Tysons Corner. Lisa, however, even after James gave her this report, remained loyal to Kowalczyk.

Zumwalt later engaged in two altercations with Kowalczyk. At an elementary school graduation for one of Zumwalt's children, the two men became physical and had to be separated. Kowalczyk, often eager to use the court system, had Zumwalt charged with assault; the charges were dropped provided that Zumwalt promised to stay away from Kowalczyk. Zumwalt convinced the judge who oversaw his divorce and custody matters to forbid Kowalczyk from staying at Lisa's home past 9 P.M. Zumwalt hired a man to watch Lisa's house. In January 1993, on a night when Kowalczyk stayed later, the man called Zumwalt. Zumwalt went to the home and confronted Kowalczyk. When Kowalczyk left, Zumwalt and the detective pursued him in two cars. Police had to intervene. Zumwalt and the detective eventually were convicted of reckless driving, but the convictions were overturned because the witness, Kowalczyk, had not been properly sworn in. The prosecutor was preparing to retry the case when Kowalczyk died.

James Zumwalt and Katherine Kowalczyk became close allies in their divorces and custody disputes with Lisa and John. The *Post* for a time reported that they were dating, but they denied any romance. Rather, they said, their friendship was based on having mutual enemies.

James Zumwalt openly hated John Kowalczyk; the two men had had public disputes that resulted in police records and James had no alibi for the night of John's death. James knew that he would be a suspect. In the company of his lawyer, he met with police. Then, on June 19, by his own account, he attempted suicide by an overdose of prescription drugs. When he awoke to find himself alive, he admitted himself to a hospital. A different news account reported that a friend found and rescued him. His lawyer admitted to the media that the episode was a suicide attempt. Both Zumwalt and his lawyer later blamed media coverage for causing terrible pressure. He told the *Post*, "We've got three generations of Zumwalts in the military service. . . All of them brought honor to the family name. I became so depressed that I kind of felt the honorable thing to do for someone who brought dishonor to the family name, even though I did nothing wrong, was to take my own life."

As the summer progressed, police moved away from Zumwalt and toward Katherine's family. The acrimony of the divorce, the disputed financial settlement, and her family's involvement all attracted police attention. Katherine had sued John on the grounds of desertion and adultery. John contested the adultery charge in court and won. She wanted $3,800 per month in child support. Because the recession had diminished John's income, the judge awarded only $608 per month, or $304 per son. The sons resisted spending time with their father, leading to more litigation about visitation rights. Katherine's father, Stanley Hyman, claimed to have spent $160,000 in legal fees on behalf of his daughter.

Stanley Hyman, age seventy at the time of the shooting, had adopted his wife's two children, though Michael spelled his surname "Highman." A former Air Force pilot, Stanley counseled military personnel on how to get jobs in the private sector. He had excellent relations with the Department of Defense. He often conducted seminars on making a successful transition into civilian businesses; he and his wife Jacqueline were facilitating such an event in Crystal City at the time of Kowalczyk's shooting. Nevertheless, police continued to see them as suspects because the Hymans owned an extensive gun collection.

The bullet that killed Kowalczyk had been encased in a sabot, plastic sheathing that prevents the grooves in the gun barrel from cutting into the bullet, thus rendering matching of the bullet to the gun almost impossible. But the type of bullet, a .30-caliber Winchester used by hunters, and what evidence they could harvest from the bullet and the wound convinced police that the weapon was a handgun known as a Thompson Center/Contender. This type of gun has interchangeable barrels up to 16 inches long, and is favored, like the .30 caliber bullet, by hunters, especially for hunting deer and other large animals. The Contender needs to be reloaded after each shot, so it was rarely involved in crimes. If it was the murder weapon, the killer had no margin for error: he had to be confident of being able to take out Kowalczyk with one shot.

Stanley Hyman allowed the police to see his many guns, including a Contender, which the police returned with a warrant to confiscate. Mrs. Hyman denied buying guns recently, but a report from the Bureau of Alcohol, Tobacco, and Firearms listed her as buying that gun in Florida on June 1. In violation of federal law, the dealer sent the gun to her through U.S. Mail. Because of the sabot, police could never rule the Hymans' Contender in or out as the murder weapon. The Hymans' lawyer defended the couple by pointing out that their invitation to the police to see the guns was a signal of innocence; a killer would not show off the murder weapon (unless the killer appeared in a story by Edgar Allan Poe).

The same weekend that James Zumwalt overdosed, the Hymans visited the Coolfont Resort in Berkeley Springs, West Virginia, roughly 120 miles from their northern Virginia home. They checked out at noon on Sunday, June 20. But that evening at about 6 P.M., Stanley called the resort to claim that on that morning about 5 A.M., he had been attacked and knocked unconscious by an intruder. His body did show cuts and bruising. The West Virginia police, who found the timing of his report strange, located no corroborating evidence.

That same weekend in Berkeley Springs, a worker at Coolfont disappeared. James Alting, age thirty-seven, left his parents' home Saturday morning. Very late Sunday night, his parents heard the car return, but James never entered the house. They found the car locked with the key inside. They called the sheriff and let a deputy search James's room. The deputy found a matchbook from the Wolf Trap Motel in Vienna, Virginia, which is near 115 Park Street, and paper with phone numbers from the 703 area code. The deputy called the numbers; at one of them, Stanley Hyman answered.

At Coolfont, Alting's frequent companion was another groundskeeper, Ralph N. Shambaugh Jr., age thirty-three, son of the county clerk and known as J.R. An avid outdoorsman, Shambaugh hunted and dressed his own game. He frequently talked with Stanley Hyman; Shambaugh's brother explained, "he always liked older people. That's his nature."

Unlike the refined Hymans, both Alting and Shambaugh had criminal records. Shambaugh had a 1979 robbery conviction and had recently been indicted for "malicious wounding," specifically, for cutting another man in the back of the neck. Alting's record included more ominous offenses: burglary, aggravated sexual assault, and a parole violation. His mother defended him and blamed his troubles on drugs: "He's a gentle-natured person. Dogs, animals, and babies like him."

At the start of August, the Hymans left for an extended vacation at a condominium in Clearwater, Florida. When Michael could not reach them, he called building security, who found the couple dead on August 4. Stanley had shot Jacqueline in the head, them himself. They left extensive letters for the police and for family members: They denied involvement in Kowalczyk's death, claimed that the glare of the investigation had greatly depressed them, explained that Stanley suffered from terrible back pain, and asserted that they chose to die together. Stanley wrote, "If I were 20 years younger, I would have the vitality to ignore the media and conduct a full-scale defense which would prove my innocence. But at age 70, I have run out of gas."

The police continued to try to link the Hymans to Alting. Just before the Hymans went to Florida, the *Post* reported than an anonymous informant had talked to police, claiming that he had been offered money to help kill Kowalczyk. This informant, plus investigation of phone records and Shambaugh's recent spending, gave Virginia police enough. On September 20, three months and ten days after the killing, a grand jury indicted Shambaugh for the murder of Kowalczyk, alleging that he was hired to do so by Stanley Hyman. How Alting might have fit in remained mysterious—perhaps he was the driver, police theorized.

On the night of June 11, 1994, near Paw Paw, West Virginia, campers found a decomposed body at the base of a 22-foot hand-dug well. The remote land belonged to Shambaugh's relatives. Despite a crushed skull, enough teeth remained for the medical examiner to compare dental records, which confirmed the body to be that of James Alting.

Robert F. Horan Jr., a prosecutor with three decades of experience, conducted the Commonwealth's case when the trial finally began in very late November 1994. The trial of Ralph Shambaugh for murder, use of a weapon, and conspiracy consumed two and half weeks and was the longest trial in the history of Fairfax

County. Many other jurisdictions routinely see capital cases last for months and would envy the swiftness of Virginia's courtroom procedures.

Horan began his case with the crime scene. Nicholas and Katherine, who now lived in California, described discovering Kowalczyk's body. Then Horan moved to his main witness: James Sabol, a worker at Coolfont, testified that Shambaugh had offered him $5,000 to help in a killing by driving the car, and had even shown Sabol a photo of the intended victim, Kowalczyk. Sabol continued that Shambaugh bragged that important people would pay $25,000 for the killing. Sabol explained, "I more or less thought we were drinking, and I thought he was playing on me. I did not actually believe he was going to do it." Sabol would not get involved, but then, according to Sabol, Shambaugh offered him $2,000 to procure a silencer or a night scope. Sabol said that he volunteered to make calls, "I wanted to make it look like I had connections. I didn't want to sound scared. I wanted to fit in." Though Shambaugh eventually said that he would not do the deed, the witness continued, Sabol became frightened on learning of Kowalczyk's death. Later in the summer, he gathered the courage to go to police.

Records and lists comprised much of the prosecution's case. After using Lisa Zumwalt to establish that Kowalczyk gravely feared Stanley Hyman, Horan submitted records of over thirty phone calls between Hyman's number and Shambaugh's calling card. On the night of the shooting, calls to Hyman's number from Shambaugh's card occurred at 7:02 P.M., 7:04 P.M., and 11:14 P.M. Then the calls ceased. A week before the killing, Shambaugh bought a cell phone at a store near Lisa Zumwalt's home. Financial records revealed that Shambaugh earned only $12,000 in 1992, but had deposited $9,000 in his bank just before the shooting. Horan also presented evidence about the gun and the sabot, linking both— though not definitively—to the Hymans. Vienna Police Chief Daniel Kerr also testified that he had selected Shambaugh's face from a photo lineup as matching someone he saw lingering at the crime scene on the night of the shooting.

Defense attorney Peter D. Greenspun utilized a multi-pronged strategy: He questioned the evidence of conspiracy, pointed to other suspects, and established an alibi. He ridiculed the alleged links between Shambaugh and Hyman. "The country bumpkin and the millionaire—it makes a good book," he said, but no evidence directly connected these people. The phone calls show contact between people at these numbers, not which people nor what they said. The Hymans' accountant testified that their accounts showed no missing funds, but he did not know if they kept money from him.

Greenspun stated, "Mr. Shambaugh absolutely denies that he killed John Kowalczyk. We're just working hard to get to the bottom of who killed John Kowalczyk. . . There remains a whole pool of suspects who had reason and opportunity." Among this pool, Greenspun chose to de-emphasize Stanley Hyman and suggest Michael Highman and James Zumwalt. Kowalczyk's sister claimed to have heard Michael outside a hearing room tell Kowalczyk, "Bang, bang," and Stanley add, "Watch your back, John." Michael denied the scene when he testified. Greenspun used James Zumwalt's private detective to narrate Zumwalt's efforts to catch Kowalczyk in misdeeds and to convince jurors that Zumwalt was obsessed with Kowalczyk. Greenspun avoided the scene from TV shows in which the defense attorney puts the other suspect on the witness stand; Greenspun circled around Zumwalt without direct confrontation. Zumwalt had been subpoenaed, but did not testify. Zumwalt, a lawyer himself, told the *Post*: "I wanted to testify. I would hope that the jury in the jury room would ask themselves, 'Why was James Zumwalt never called as a witness by the defense if he was their prime suspect?' Mr. Greenspun didn't want me on the stand because he knew for a fact that I had not done it and had passed a polygraph."

Finally, Greenspun produced several family members and friends who placed Shambaugh in West Virginia at his home on the night of the killing. Shambaugh did not testify.

The lawyers gave Alting only fleeting references. The judge ruled that they could say that he was dead, but not how he died. The lawyers chose not to complicate the case by lingering over his possible role.

The jury members were largely well-educated professionals, including, according to the *Post*, "two lawyers, two teachers, a Federal Express Corp. employee and two [military] defense consultants." After twelve hours, the jury returned a partial verdict, guilty of conspiracy. They deadlocked on the other two charges—murder and use of the weapon—but planned to keep working. Horan suggested that the jury be given the option of debating if Shambaugh was an accessory to murder, which was not one of the original charges. Greenspun objected, and the judge ruled that giving that choice at this late time would seem to be directing the jury from the bench on what to decide, and he did not want to appear to be steering the verdict. After twenty total hours, the jury remained deadlocked.

Two jurors, a Fairfax city councilman and a lawyer, described the deliberations for the press. The jury accepted the evidence of conspiracy, but resisted convicting of murder. The jury wanted more direct proof that Shambaugh was on the scene and pulled the trigger. One juror said, perhaps not realizing the pun, "You're always looking for a smoking gun, and that was certainly lacking." The first vote was 7-5 to convict, and the last vote was 8-4, showing how little sides had changed during discussion.

Shambaugh received an eighteen-year sentence for the conspiracy charge. Horan planned to retry him, this time as an accomplice, a charge that Horan felt would have a better chance of conviction. But on March 8, 1995, as the retrial was about to begin, the sides came to a plea deal: "accessory before the fact," a lesser charge, but one with significant prison time. The lawyers found the deal reasonable given the evidence and the risk on both sides. Yet both maintained their positions. Horan told the press that he was sure that Shambaugh was the shooter, while Greenspun insisted that Shambaugh was not at 115 Park that day. The judge sentenced Shambaugh to thirty-five years, to be served concurrently with the conspiracy sentence.

The case ended as it did because the Northern Virginia jurors insisted on a high standard of proof. The records convinced them that a conspiracy existed, but its existence was not enough for them to cross over to convicting for murder. They demanded direct evidence of personal involvement in the actual killing. This demand contrasts with what little evidence jurors in other parts of Virginia needed to convict in cases discussed in a later chapter.

Under the parole rules of the time, which have since been made much tougher, Shambaugh was eligible for parole and likely to be released on June 26, 2011. However, on July 21, 2005, a mandatory drug test came back positive for marijuana. As this violation seriously jeopardized the parole date, Shambaugh appealed the disciplinary finding to the warden, into state court, and eventually into federal court. Representing himself, Shambaugh claimed that he was denied due process in that he could not procure defense witnesses, that the cup used in the test was defective, that the procedures were not followed, and that he was denied a full court hearing on the evidence. The federal district court wrote on September 29, 2008, that the prison system followed its procedures for drug tests and for giving Shambaugh time to request witnesses. The court dismissed Shambaugh's suit, and his new mandatory parole date is June 3, 2017.

CHAPTER 8

Confessions:
Earl Washington Jr., 1983-2007;
The Norfolk Four, 1997-2009;
and Beverly Monroe, 1992-2003

Regarding the cases in this chapter, readers might consider people and events from earlier chapters as touchstones. Joseph Horgas, the police detective who tracked down Timothy Spencer, emphasized physical and scientific evidence, developed patterns based on the series of crimes, and felt undeterred by a previous confession in a related case. He trusted the empirical. The investigators in the shooting of John Kowalczyk, along with Commonwealth Attorney Robert Horan, crafted a case based on a network of interlocking clues: financial transactions, phone records, and gun purchases. In this case, the police did not immediately seize a logical suspect who lacked an alibi, James Zumwalt. They interviewed him with his lawyer present and developed evidence well beyond interviews before accusing anyone.

In the cases that follow, the contrasts will be apparent and disturbing.

In a groundbreaking journal article from 1998, sociology professors Richard A. Leo and Richard J. Ofshe collected sixty recent cases of "false confessions"—instances in which a suspect gave a confession at odds with the evidence yet still was charged. Eccentric attention-seekers often confess to crimes; the authors completely discount these situations to focus on cases in which the confessed suspect was actually charged with the crime. Leo and Ofshe try to set a high standard: "only cases in which the defendant's confession is not supported by any physical or reliable inculpatory evidence." In analyzing what conditions brought about these confessions, Leo and Ofshe disclose troubling police behaviors and judicial attitudes.

Some police trust that their psychological techniques can wrest confessions from suspects. Training manuals along with popular TV shows (such as the 1990s show *Homicide: Life on the Street* and, from the 2000s, *The Closer*) share this confident attitude and lionize officers who are effective at getting confessions. The textbook *Fundamentals of Criminal Investigation* (6th edition, 1994), by Charles E. O'Hara and Gregory L. O'Hara, includes these lines: "The ability to obtain information by questioning is the most prized talent of the investigator. . . The guilty person is in possession of most of the information necessary for a successful prosecution, and if he is questioned intelligently, he can usually be induced to talk. . . It will be found that if the accused can be induced to 'talk' the prospects of a successful prosecution are usually bright." Prosecutors, judges, and the public at large have trouble believing that an innocent person would confess to a crime, short of torture. Yet Leo and Ofshe elaborate sixty cases where innocent people did confess. To describe the power of a confession, the authors state, "Once a confession is obtained, investigation often ceases, and convicting the defendant becomes the only goal of both investigators and prosecutors." This sentence directly applies to the cases that follow.

Two of the article's sixty cases are from Virginia: those of David Vasquez (who appeared in a previous chapter) and Earl Washington Jr.

The Case of Earl Washington Jr., 1983–2007

Earl Washington Jr. was born in 1960 near Culpeper to a black family that had been laborers for over a hundred years. Washington attended school for nine years, the last five in special education. An eventual IQ test gave him a score of 69, in the range of mild retardation.

On the night of May 21, 1983, after a bout of drinking and an argument with his brother about a woman, Washington, age twenty-three, went to the nearby home of Hazel Weeks, age seventy-eight. There he took a gun that he had seen in her kitchen. When she awoke and surprised him, he bashed her over the head with a wooden chair, causing significant bleeding. He wanted money; she pointed out her purse, and he left with money. He later shot his brother in the foot with the gun and hid in a grassy field where he was apprehended a few hours later, still in possession of the gun.

Washington confessed to these events quite readily and signed a statement written for him. His version largely matches Mrs. Weeks' version of the crime. But the police used no taping for this confession nor for what would follow. Sheriff's Investigator Terry Schrum then asked Washington about other local violent break-ins. Washington waived his rights, signed the form, then agreed after some reluctance that he had done other misdeeds, once Schrum mentioned them. Journalist Margaret Edds writes in *An Expendable Man* (2003): "Before the interrogations ended over a couple of days, he had confessed to three break-ins, two malicious woundings, one attempted rape, two actual rapes, two robberies, burglary, and capital murder—every crime about which he was asked." The capital murder confession began when Schrum asked, "Earl, did you kill that girl in Culpeper?"

That girl in Culpeper was Rebecca Williams, age nineteen, who died brutally on June 4, 1982. A married mother of three, she suffered rape and stabbing inside her apartment just before midday. Two of her infant children were in the apartment at the time. She struggled to the outside door and collapsed in a bloodied heap. She told rescuers that a single black man whom she did not know had attacked her. She lived just two more hours. The case went cold.

Schrum brought in State Police Agent Reese Wilmore, who took notes and eventually produced a transcript. Washington confessed not in a narrative but in a question-and-answer sequence with Wilmore. Washington first said that Williams was black, then said white under more questioning. Police took him on a tour of apartment complexes; he claimed that none looked familiar. At Williams's complex, when Washington allegedly hesitated, Wilmore simply asked which apartment was hers; Washington pointed in the other direction.

Washington quickly recanted all his confessions, except for the attack on Mrs. Weeks. Authorities never pressed charges on the other matters, except for the cold case involving Rebecca Williams. As early as 1983, the irony was clear: On almost all the cases, Washington's confessions were unbelievable, yet police chose to believe him about Williams. How could Washington get into this terrible situation? His lawyer in the Weeks matter, Jonathan Lynn, told Edds, "Earl was like a little child or anyone who wants to please. . . I realized early on in talking to Earl that I had to be very careful as to how I phrased my questions. If he felt my question was begging a particular answer, I may well get that answer."

Washington's family pooled their resources and hired, with NAACP assistance, John Scott, a black civil rights attorney with no experience in capital cases. Doctors examined Washington and declared him competent to stand trial and to have waived his rights. So the trial took place on January 18 through 20, 1984. In defense, Scott put Washington on the witness stand; he denied doing the deed and giving the confession. Scott seemed to have gambled that seeing Washington on the stand would convince jurors of his disability. Edds unsubtly charges that Scott was out of his element: "Bennett [the prosecutor] called fourteen witnesses, and their testimony and cross-examination was 162 pages long. Scott called two . . . their remarks filled 27 pages. Bennett's closing covered nine pages of transcript; Scott's two." The jury, which included two black members, took fifty minutes to convict. They recommended execution.

Scott stayed with Washington through the unsuccessful state appeals. The state funded no lawyers for federal appeals, so Washington languished in prison as his execution date approached. In a dramatic and now famous scene, on August 14, 1985, a young attorney visited Mecklenburg prison to consult with Joe Giarratano, a fascinating inmate in his own right. Convicted of double murder and under death sentence, Giarratano was preparing on his own a class-action lawsuit to compel the Commonwealth to fund attorneys for the federal appeals of indigent death row inmates. Giarratano had placed Washington's name prominently as his chief example. When the lawyer sat before him, Giarratano snapped, "Earl Washington has an IQ of 69, an execution date three weeks away, and no lawyer. What the hell are you going to do about it?"

The young lawyer convinced her New York City firm, Paul, Weiss, Rifkind, Wharton & Garrison, to work on the case. Writing furiously, Eric Freedman crafted a habeas corpus petition to address constitutional issues. Scott cooperated and sent them his materials from the case, including the trial record. With nine days to spare, the firm delivered the petition to a judge in Culpeper, expecting that he would deny the stay and they would have to race to federal court. Instead, the judge granted the stay without protest.

The firm associated with Virginia trial lawyer Robert Hall, who combed through the actual evidence. He noted that police had recovered semen from Williams's body and from a blue blanket in her home. The technology of the time allowed the semen on the blanket to be tested to determine blood type. Washington's blood type did not match. Scott had overlooked this crucial evidence. So the amended habeas petition to federal court addressed the scientific evidence and the dubious confession.

District Court passed on the case, but the Circuit Court allowed a full hearing, held in June 1990. In December 1991, by a 3-0 vote, the court sent the case back to District Court for a hearing on the blood evidence. (On the federal bench, only a district court can take evidence and hear from witnesses.) The ensuing hearing featured the scientific discussion of possible sources of a semen stain on a blanket, of the blood type in the semen, and if other biological fluids could mask the blood type. The judge ruled that the failure to pursue this evidence at trial was not a reversible error, nor even an error. The Circuit Court affirmed 2-1.

As the lawyers planned to continue the federal appeals, in 1993 Stephen D. Rosenthal became Virginia's Attorney General to fill out the term of Mary Sue Terry, who was running for governor. Intrigued by the new DNA evidence, Rosenthal and his top deputy, Gail Sterling Marshall, who would later represent Jens Soering, considered applying DNA technology to the Washington case. In October 1993, DNA test results largely excluded Washington. But the Commonwealth would not budge, suggesting contrary to all previous testimony and evidence that Washington may have had an accomplice. Due to hedges about degrees of probability in the findings, the state argued that the tests did not absolutely exclude Washington.

The lawyers then chose a path fraught with great risk. They deliberately missed the deadline for a federal court filing and used the scientific evidence to ask outgoing governor L. Douglas Wilder for clemency. With the advent of DNA evidence in the case, the Innocence Project, a nationwide organization that seeks to use scientific evidence in appeals of criminal cases, consulted with the lawyers and eventually became deeply involved. On his last full day in office, January 14, 1994, Wilder commuted Washington's death sentence to life. He did not issue a pardon. Thankful to be able to stay alive, Washington accepted the offer.

Washington's family seldom contacted him, due to the vast distances between their homes and the prison and due to their (and his) limited literacy. Though he admitted to loneliness and some frustrations about his case, Washington never complained of his treatment in prison, neither by guards nor inmates. Other convicts of limited intellect and passive personality, such as David Vasquez and the Norfolk Four's Joseph Dick, suffered gravely within prison walls. Race may be part of the reason for Washington's relatively benign treatment. Washington was a black former laborer with some size and strength, so the largely black inmate population left him be. His cheerful and friendly nature also kept him out of quarrels and in others' good graces. This good nature also won him several protectors, "stickmen" in prison parlance, among them Joe Giarratano. Washington earned an almost perfect conduct score, so guards had no reason to hassle him. In this bleak and dangerous environment, his traits proved to be assets.

His lawyers had never received the actual DNA results. A documentary filmmaker did obtain them, and her 2000 documentary for TV's *Frontline* exposed that the results almost certainly excluded Washington. The invigorated lawyers agitated for the newer, more sophisticated DNA tests and for the governor to consider clemency. As had occurred decades before with the case of the Martinsville Seven, print and TV journalists drew national attention to Virginia's procedures, in this instance to Virginia's reluctance to act on behalf of an inmate whom science seemed to exonerate. Gov. James Gilmore ordered the most up-to-date DNA tests on both samples, from within Williams's body and from the blanket. The tests excluded Washington, and at last, on October 2, 2000, Gilmore pardoned Washington. Gilmore, however, did not order Washington's release: Washington had to serve the remainder of his time for the attack on Mrs. Weeks. The state parole board allowed him to go free on February 12, 2001.

Gilmore's pardon message reflected a reluctance to admit that the prosecution of Washington was wrong:

> I am deeply sympathetic to the pain and anguish already suffered by the family and friends of Rebecca Williams, and I regret any reliving of that pain that these events may cause. . . In my judgment, a jury afforded the benefit of the DNA evidence and analysis available to me today would have reached a different conclusion regarding the guilt of Earl Washington. . . It is important for the public to understand that absence of DNA evidence does not necessarily mean an individual is absent from the crime scene—just that he has not left any DNA markers.

Washington's lawyers remained bitter that neither Governor Wilder nor Governor Gilmore could take the step of apologizing to a man who had been wrongly convicted. On the day of Washington's release, Eric Freedman, who had worked on the appeals, told the press, "In anything like a system of justice, the governor should have been here at the front door of the prison."

To make the release palatable to Gilmore, the lawyers arranged for Washington to be transitioned into supervised care in Virginia Beach. He gradually learned employable skills in maintenance and carpet cleaning and earned a job. He had trouble with contracts (such as leases), checkbooks, and banking; his mental limitations required continued supervision. He married a mildly retarded woman in 2002.

In 2006, a federal jury awarded Washington $2.25 million from the estate of Agent Wilmore, who had coaxed the false confession from Washington. Among Washington's attorneys were Peter Neufeld of the Innocence Project and Robert Hall, who stayed with the case through the years. The trial began dramatically: The Commonwealth, which funded Wilmore's defense because Wilmore was a state employee, stipulated that Washington was innocent in the death of Rebecca Williams. Indeed, the DNA from the scene matched that of an offender already in custody. Neufeld presented to the jury the following argument: Washington had no role in the crime; yet after questioning by Wilmore, Washington gave a confession that included details of the crime; those details could only have originated from Wilmore. Hence, Wilmore fabricated the confession. After the trial, Virginia officials negotiated a payout of $1.9 million. Trustees would administer the funds for Washington.

In July 2010, the Innocence Project listed eleven inmates from Virginia as having been cleared due to DNA evidence. The list included David Vasquez and Earl Washington.

Journalists credit the pressure and attention brought to Virginia due to nationwide publicity over the Washington case with leading to significant new laws. In 2001, Virginia liberalized its infamous twenty-one-days-after-sentencing limitation on the presentation of new evidence. That same year, a new law allowed DNA tests to be requested directly by inmates at any time. A 2004 law allowed appeals, also at any time, based on newly discovered scientific evidence.

The Norfolk Four, 1997–2009

On July 8, 1997, William "Billy" Bosko, age nineteen, an enlisted sailor, returned to his Norfolk apartment after a week at sea. His wife, Michelle Moore-Bosko, age eighteen, lay dead in the bedroom, violated, stabbed, and choked. She had blood, presumably from her attacker, under her fingernails. In addition to this blood, her attacker left his semen in her body and on a blanket.

In the era of DNA, citizens might expect this biological evidence to be pivotal and definitive. But this was not how police and prosecutors treated it. The following account employs the book on the case by Tom Wells and Richard A. Leo, *The Wrong Guys* (2008), retrospective journalism, and the federal court opinion on the case.

Screams from the distraught husband brought neighbors out of their apartments to assist. Two were Tamika Taylor, who in a short time had become close to Michelle, and Danial Williams, age twenty-five, who was also in the navy. Taylor volunteered to the two detectives who were put on the case that Williams often tried to encounter Michelle and frequently visited her. The detectives, Maureen Evans and Scott Halverson, asked Williams to come to the station; they told him that as he had been one of the first neighbors at the scene, that he could give them vital information.

Several factors made Williams an odd suspect. He had a new wife of only ten days, and she was suffering from cancer and needed a lot of attention. She died four months later. He had a friend living with them in the apartment, Joseph Dick Jr., age twenty, another enlisted sailor. And Williams's parents were visiting, staying nearby. Nonetheless, the detectives planned to subject him to a forceful interrogation.

Evans and Halverson took notes but did not tape record the questioning. Williams arrived at the station about 6:30 P.M., but he was not put in the interrogation room until 8:00 P.M. He signed forms waiving his rights. Within thirty minutes, the detectives accused him of being interested in Michelle. At 9:45 P.M. he took a polygraph; he passed, or showed no signs of deception; they told him that he had failed and was lying. After 4:30 A.M., police brought in Detective

Robert Glenn Ford. At 7:00 A.M., detectives tape recorded Williams confessing to rape and murder.

As the years went on, advocates of the Norfolk Four would vilify Ford. He did take over the case as lead detective. Yet Evans and Halverson bear responsibility for the very early decision to bring in Williams for questioning based on Taylor's statement and for the decision to become accusatory. And two prosecutors, Valerie Bowen and D. J. Hansen, accepted the evidence that Ford provided and used it in court. Accountability in this case spreads to a number of officials.

Williams's confession did not match the crime scene. He claimed that the attack began in the living room, but that room and the hallway were undisturbed. The orderly state of the apartment, including undisturbed papers on a hallway shelf, would become major points of evidence. Williams claimed that he had struck Michelle with a hard shoe; he said nothing about knife wounds nor strangulation. Nonetheless, police stopped investigating: They never even searched Williams's apartment for evidence such as bloody clothes.

Within days, Williams recanted his confession. In December, the Virginia Division of Forensic Science's Central Laboratory revealed that Williams's DNA did not match the biological material harvested at the scene.

At this point, the case became a gruesome sequence of falling dominos. Detectives decided that Williams must have had an accomplice, despite the confession, the orderly crime scene, and the single contributor of DNA at the scene. They selected Williams's roommate, Joseph Dick. On January 12, 1998, Detective Ford and his partner pulled Dick off his ship for questioning, which began at 10:10 A.M. He waived his rights and took a polygraph, which he passed; Ford told him that he failed. A bit after 2 P.M., Dick confessed to helping Williams murder Michelle. Ford quizzed him about specifics and finally turned on a tape recorder at 5:18 P.M.

The next day, Dick recanted. He would claim that he was on duty the night of the murder, and officers confirmed the alibi with book authors Wells and Leo. But these officers did not come forward in a timely manner to rescue Dick, and the ship's records from the night were not available. Throughout the coming years, Dick would give multiple versions of that night.

Most who dealt with Dick suggested that he possessed only limited intelligence; his family told Wells and Leo that they were surprised that the navy accepted him. He had trouble with directions and performed his duties best if tightly supervised. He was socially awkward, given to staring, and usually sullen. Given these traits and his slight build, Dick had a difficult time in jail and later in prison. In March 1998, police learned that Dick's DNA did not match.

Dick wrote bizarre letters from jail, sometimes expressing affection for Williams's wife. One letter said that a sailor named Eric from a particular ship should be beaten. So on April 8, 1998, at 10:20 A.M., Ford began to question Eric Wilson, age twenty-one. Wilson waived his rights; he took a polygraph, and Ford told him that he failed. At 7:05 P.M., Wilson's confession to rape was tape recorded. (Wells and Leo speculate that the confession focused on rape because detectives wanted to account for the DNA, as Williams and Dick had already admitted to murder.)

On April 27, 1998, with his attorney, Ford, and a prosecutor present, Dick amended his statement to include Wilson in the attack on Michelle. In June, police learned that Wilson's DNA did not match.

On June 16, Dick amended his story again to include a gang of attackers, some whom he did not know. On June 18, a detective called a woman who had visited Williams in jail and asked about Williams's close friends. She gave them the name Derek Tice, a man who had also visited Williams in jail. Dick then picked Tice from a book of sailors' photos. So police selected Tice, as they had selected Wilson and Dick, on the most tenuous of links and in contrast to the orderly scene that suggested a sole perpetrator.

Tice, age twenty-eight, had left the navy and was living in Florida. That very night, June 18, local police surrounded his home and arrested him.

On June 25, in Norfolk, Ford talked with Tice, starting at 2:15 P.M. Ford lied several times, which is legal for police to do. He said that others had named Tice as an attacker and would testify, and that physical evidence placed him at the scene. Predictably, Ford added that Tice had failed a polygraph, which the operator claimed that Tice did. Polygraphs measure emotional response, and Tice was in an emotional state. By evening, Tice confessed, claiming that six men were involved. Ford did not begin the taping until 11:39 P.M.

Note the contrasts with earlier cases. When investigating the murders of the Haysoms, Det. Ricky Gardner taped everything, thus establishing a record of his contacts with people and their stories. In Norfolk, Ford and other police took only written notes. They did not tape until late in the process, after the suspect had been interrogated for hours and had his confession refined by continued questioning. The tapes are final drafts of stories that were crafted from hours of work. In addition, in the Martinsville rape case, police felt confident in their case because all seven suspects separately confessed, giving similar stories. Ruby Floyd was too traumatized to say how many men attacked her. The men themselves consistently put that number at seven. Mrs. Floyd said that assaults came in two waves; the confessions matched this claim. In Norfolk, each confession differed not only in specifics of the attack (such as how the victim was violated), but also in the number of attackers.

Tice gave the names of two additional men and later a third. Police arrested them, but the confessions ceased. Richard Pauley, the first, was an unlikely choice to have joined with Williams in anything because he, Pauley, was the ex-husband of Williams's wife. He stuck to his alibi that he was on the computer and phone to Australia that night, verified by bills and logs. Geoffrey Alan Farris was the next man. Ford was on vacation when Pauley was arrested, but he did interrogate Farris, who withstood the pressure and refused to confess. The third man, whom Tice gave up later, was John Danser, who was living near Philadelphia and had work reports and ATM receipts to bolster his alibi.

DNA from Tice did not match, nor from the three men whom Tice named.

Lawyers for Williams and Dick negotiated pleas for their clients; a key motivation for the pleas was to avoid the death sentences that trials could bring.

On February 22, 1999, the mother of Tamika Taylor gave police a letter from Omar Ballard, who was in prison on a rape charge for an attack that occurred ten days after the attack on Michelle. By a terrible irony, two weeks before Michelle's death, Billy Bosko had given Ballard haven in the apartment when a mob was chasing him, accusing him of a rape, and calling racial slurs. (Ballard was black. The Boskos and the arrested men were white.) In the letter, Ballard expressed anger that the letter's recipients, whom he thought were his friends, had not written to him in prison, adding, "the next morning Michelle got killed. Guess who did that. *Me*, ha, ha. It was not the first time. I'm good ain't I."

Ballard's DNA matched the DNA at the crime scene. On March 4, and again on March 11, Ballard told Ford—on tape—that he had attacked Michelle alone. He taunted Ford with a line that became infamous: "Them four people that opened their mouths is stupid."

But the dominos continued to fall. The judge would not allow Williams to withdraw his plea. Tice totally disavowed his confessions, and he and Wilson demanded trials. Tice had provided the only evidence against Pauley, Farris, and Danser, so police released them. Pauley and Farris had spent ten months in jail, Danser seven. Dick held to his story, or rather to his most recent version.

At trial, Wilson was found guilty of rape but not of murder and sentenced to eight and a half years. Tice endured two trials. Ballard either refused to testify or denied involvement at Wilson's and Tice's trials. Dick testified for the prosecution in all three. In February 2000, Tice was found guilty of rape and murder and sentenced to life. The Virginia Court of Appeals reversed the conviction because the judge had improperly instructed the jury about whether capital murder applied only to the immediate killer—it did, but the judge said that capital murder could be broader—and because the judge limited the questioning of Ballard. On retrial, in January 2003, the jury again convicted.

When the habeas corpus appeal for this second conviction reached federal District Court, Judge Richard L. Williams wrote a devastating critique of the evidence and of the power of the confession. (Judge Williams had earlier written a pivotal opinion in Beverly Monroe's case, to be discussed next.) In an opinion dated September 14, 2009, Judge Williams points out that the Commonwealth called only six witnesses. Four referred to the crime scene without reference to Tice. Of this crime scene, Judge Williams writes, "Indeed, the physical evidence tended to refute the theory that the rape and murder had been committed by multiple individuals. . . there was remarkably little sign of such violent activity by so many men in such a confined space."

The other two witnesses were Ford and Dick. Judge Williams enumerates five different versions of Dick's story: "Confronted with the history of the meandering development of Dick's account of the crime and Dick's expressed willingness to tell the police anything they wanted to hear, a juror would have significant questions about the veracity of Dick's testimony." If the physical evidence and Dick's testimony weighed in Tice's favor, his confession weighed against him, verified by Ford, but Williams quotes this line from the polygraph operator's notes: "He [Tice] told me he decide not to say any more, that he might decide to after he talks with a lawyer, or spends some time alone thinking about it. I told him he would be given time to think about it. He *did not* request a lawyer." Williams reads the line as a request for a lawyer, rules that Tice's lawyer should have moved at trial to suppress the confession, and that the confession was taken in violation of Tice's rights. If the confession is inadmissible, no credible evidence would be left, in Judge Williams's analysis.

Between 2003 and Judge Williams's ruling in 2009, the case inspired vigorous debate. The facts belied an easy explanation: that four men could confess, recant, and be declared guilty for a crime in which the DNA evidence pointed to a lone fifth man. Dick did eventually repudiate his confessions and return to his original story, that he was on duty that night. Between 2006 and 2008, the *Washington Post* printed six editorials calling for the governor to intervene in the case and consider pardons for the Norfolk Four. On January 12, 2008, four former Attorneys General of Virginia called for clemency. On November 11, 2008, thirty retired FBI agents from the area joined the calls for pardons.

In July 2009, lawyer turned author John Grisham expressed interest in the case as a possible screenplay. In his research on an earlier book, Grisham had allied himself with the Innocence Project, which was helping some of the Norfolk defendants. Grisham especially admired the book by Wells and Leo. Living near Charlottesville and frequently contributing to Democratic Party causes, Grisham had access to Governor Timothy M. Kaine. When Kaine finally acted, Grisham admitted to the press, "The Governor is an old ally of mine, and I know he does not discuss clemency with anyone. Still, several months ago we had a glass of wine. . . Let's put it this way. I feel sure he read the book."

On August 6, 2009, Kaine granted conditional pardons to three of the Norfolk Four—Williams, Dick, and Tice. He excepted Wilson, who had completed his sentence for rape. Kaine wrote:

> The effect of these Conditional Pardons is to reduce the sentences of the Petitioners to time served. . . These Conditional Pardons are not a conclusive finding of innocence but rather a reduction of sentences . . .
>
> I find that the combined weight of all the evidence in this case does not conclusively exonerate the Petitioners from any possibility of involvement in the rape and murder of Michele Bosko. Instead, the Petitioners have demonstrated, through the accumulation of all the evidence now known, that any involvement in the crime was of a significantly lesser magnitude than that of the primary perpetrator, Omar Ballard.

As with Governor Gilmore and Earl Washington, Governor Kaine would not declare the Norfolk Four to be "the wrong guys." Derek Tice received some approbation of his innocence the following month when Judge Williams vacated his conviction.

John and Carol Moore, Michelle's parents, released a statement condemning the pardon, directing special ire toward Grisham for using his influence:

Our family is devastated to learn that Governor Kaine has chosen to ignore the facts and history of this case by granting a conditional pardon to these confessed and convicted rapists and murderers. There is absolutely zero new evidence or information to justify this decision. . . It is truly shameful and a disservice to the citizens of Virginia and our family, that the decisions of the courts have been ignored, and confessed rapists and murderers are being set free.

Advocates of the Norfolk Four wondered why Michelle's family stubbornly clung to a belief that was illogical according to the evidence. Two reasons, one general and the other very specific, may explain their tenacity. In general, families of crime victims often bond with and trust the authorities. And in this particular case, the family experienced hearing the very detailed taped confessions. That these tapes resulted from hours of preparation and coaching by police can explain why the tapes were so vivid and detailed. This vividness perhaps rendered them too emotional for the family to doubt.

The Case of Beverly Monroe, 1992–2003

Earl Washington possessed only limited intelligence. The Norfolk Four were enlisted men trained to be trusting of authority. These explanations for why they would consent to interviews and then confess to crimes while in police custody do not apply to Beverly Monroe. She had earned bachelor's and master's degrees in the sciences and worked in the patent office of Philip Morris. One of her daughters had earned a law degree and was working for a judge on Virginia's Court of Appeals. That Beverly Monroe would agree to a long police interrogation and then confess and then vehemently recant demonstrates the power of questioning, yet also raises troubling issues about the relationship between citizens and the police.

The following narrative about Beverly Monroe draws from retrospective press accounts, the book *The Count and the Confession* (2002) by John Taylor, and from the federal court decision that finally resolved the case, or resolved at least its legal dimensions.

On the morning of March 5, 1992, Beverly Monroe and an estate worker discovered Roger de la Burde in his library, dead from a gunshot to the head. The setting was Windsor, a 220-acre farm in Powhatan County near Richmond. Windsor's history went back to the 1600s. Beverly had dined with Burde the evening before. She told police that she had called him later when she returned home to Richmond—she said that they would call each other after visits to assure that they made it home safely. She got a busy signal throughout the night. Worried, she claimed, she returned to the estate in the morning. The house was locked, but the caretaker forced open a sliding door. They found Burde lying on his side on his sofa, a bullethole in the front of his head. The caretaker moved the hands and the gun to feel for a pulse. The following clues appeared at the scene: the placement of the body, the position of the hands and the stains on the fingers, ashes from paper in the fireplace, and two Marlboro cigarette butts in a nearby ashtray. The original position of the gun remained in dispute throughout the case.

No theory of what occurred ever accounted for the burned paper nor for the cigarette butts. The stains on the fingers would lead to wrangling among experts throughout the next ten years. But on this day as he surveyed the scene and bagged the hands for testing, Sheriff Greg Neal considered the case to be a probable suicide.

Burde and Beverly, ages sixty and fifty-four respectively in March 1992, had been romantically involved for thirteen years. They met at Philip Morris, where Burde, a Ph.D. in chemistry, had helped to invent a process that expanded tobacco while also cutting down on the dangerous substances it contained. He had testified for Philip Morris in a successful lawsuit against another tobacco company for unauthorized use of the process. These events seemed to show Burde's value to the company, but he had testy relationships with superiors and they pushed him into early retirement. He sued the company, claiming that for his testimony he was due, by agreement, a small percentage of the massive profits that the process generated for Philip Morris.

As an expensive sidelight, Burde collected art, specializing in African and modern sculptures. He claimed that many of his African pieces came to him from his father; a New York curator exposed that they were taken by Burde in the 1960s in violation of

Nigerian law. Burde had also tried to suborn friendly local artists to make copies of modern sculptures based on photographs, and Burde would pass them off as real. Burde placed statues and paintings in his barn and exposed them to weather so that his claims of their age would look convincing. He donated seventy-two pieces to Radford University, where his daughter went to college, and the donations included some fakes. In a magazine article that accompanied the bequest, he gave himself a French lineage, but his story contained multiple historical inaccuracies. The truth of his life was significant in its own right: He defected from Communist Poland by surreptitiously crossing the border during a trip to East Berlin.

These roguish, tempestuous traits were equally apparent in Burde's personal life. A divorced father of two grown daughters, Burde juggled multiple affairs. Indeed, just before his death, according to trial testimony, he engaged with one of his other mistresses to bring a new woman by his house. He had begun, in 1990 or early 1991, an affair with the younger Dr. Krystyna Drewnowska, a biochemist at the Medical College of Virginia, and she had become pregnant. The couple had earlier visited a doctor to ask about sex selection: Burde wanted a male heir. Drewnowska had drafted an agreement of support, regardless of the baby's sex, but Burde had yet to sign it at the time of his death. On February 27, 1992, days before the shooting, Drewnowska learned from doctors that the child would be a girl. Whether Burde knew this fact or not would be contested at trial. As a further complication, Drewnowska had an estranged husband, Wojtek Drewnowska, who had tried to repay Burde for the adultery by telling the state police about the faked art.

Beverly knew about Krystyna Drewnowska; she had even seen the draft of the support agreement. Throughout the case, people wondered how she could stay with such a rogue. She had been married before, and Burde had grown close to her three children, just as Beverly felt close to Burde's daughter Corinna, who lived in the area. Beverly enjoyed her visits to Windsor, and Burde's will gave her the right to reside there until her death, when it would pass to Corinna. They both enjoyed art exhibitions and the Richmond social scene: On February 29, 1992, Burde and Beverly's family attended a ball at the Virginia Museum of Fine Arts. Perhaps the simplest explanation will suffice: Beverly treasured her time with Burde, and she had decided that these times more than compensated for his darker aspects.

If Burde committed suicide, the many complications of his life would be factors in his choice, but if Burde had been murdered, at least three suspects were obvious: Beverly and both Drewnowskas.

The state police investigator called into the case formed a theory early on that Burde had been murdered and that Beverly, as the last person to see him alive and as the more aggrieved of his two main mistresses, was the probable shooter. Senior Agent Dave Riley entered the case initially to apprise Sheriff Neal of the state's investigation about the forged art. Riley found the awkward position of Burde's body unusual for a suicide. Krystyna Drewnowska had been urging the police to consider murder and had given them, through an attorney, an undated letter from Beverly to Burde complaining about his relationship with Drewnowska. Then Drewnowska left America for eight weeks. Riley convened a meeting with the medical examiner's specialists, including then–deputy chief Dr. Marcella Fierro. The group discussed whether Burde could have held the gun upside down, how an impression of the gun seemed to appear in his right hand, and how to explain the stains on the fingers. The group tentatively agreed on murder, pending further testing.

Armed with this official sanction for his theory, but still lacking convincing evidence of anyone's guilt, Riley plotted to surprise Beverly and perhaps get an incriminating admission. On the morning of March 26, 1992, they met at Windsor to discuss her relationship with Burde and how she found the body. Riley then asked if she would take a polygraph test, suggesting that it was a routine matter that could be accomplished that very day. She agreed. Without stopping to eat, she went to the nearby state police divisional headquarters for the test.

Unlike several of the Norfolk Four, Beverly's polygraph results indicated deception to questions about being at the scene and having shot Burde. Polygraphs measure emotional responses, so her upset state could explain her reaction. Regardless, unlike Detective Ford in

Norfolk, Riley did not lie to his quarry about her results. With two secretaries observing but without activating the recording device, he asked her to account for the results. The secretaries' notes, referred to at length in the Federal District Court opinion on the case, detail that Beverly denied being present when Burde died and insisted upon her earlier story. Riley suggested that maybe she had been there during the suicide and blocked the experience, and he offered that he himself had blocked memories of witnessing his father's suicide. Beverly's father's death had been a suicide, so the story may have had emotional impact. For whatever reason, she admitted to the memory of being there when Burde shot himself. Riley had employed an interrogation technique in which a suspect is convinced to admit to a small but incriminating aspect as an entree into greater admissions. After ninety minutes, Riley activated the tape and asked her to review her new version. In less than twenty minutes, he interrupted her forty-seven times, yet got her to admit that she was present.

Desiring a second confession to an outside party, Riley urged her to tell Corinna what happened, once Beverly felt that she could. So over a lunch on April 1, Beverly told Corinna that she now recalled being present when Burde died.

Beverly's son Gavin, a college student, had recalled her coming home the night of Burde's death around 10 P.M. As Burde had made a call to his publisher—he was working on a book about African art—about that time (whether it was 10 or 10:30 would be disputed at length), Gavin supplied his mother with a solid alibi. Riley neutralized him by getting him to admit that he did not look at the clock when Beverly returned.

By the start of June, the Medical Examiner's Office had conducted tests with clay hands and dummy heads and concluded that Burde had been murdered. But the Commonwealth Attorney, Jack Lewis, was not ready to move to arrest Beverly. So Riley sought to get Beverly to incriminate herself anew. On June 3, he called her at her office at Philip Morris and insisted that they meet. He suggested a secluded Civil War park, Drewry's Bluff. Without wearing a wire, he bluffed her with the claim that the prosecutor would bring charges against her because the cause of Burde's death would not be ruled a suicide, because Beverly had motive, and because Beverly was there and claimed it was suicide. Over two hours, they crafted a fragmented, list-style statement in which Beverly confirmed that she was there when Burde killed himself. Riley wrote out the statement; Beverly signed and dated it.

That night, Beverly finally consulted with her daughter Katie, an attorney, who after becoming enraged at both her mother for being foolish and the police for their tactics, mobilized the family to procure a seasoned criminal defense attorney for what would surely follow. They settled on Richmond lawyer Murray Janus. Beverly vehemently reverted to her original story. On June 9, Commonwealth Attorney Lewis procured a grand jury indictment against Beverly for first-degree murder and use of a firearm.

In a controversial move, Janus chose not to object to the admission of the confessions into evidence on the grounds that the confessions were coerced. The hearing for motions would occur in open court in front of the press, and would lead to discussion of the "failed" polygraph. Polygraph tests are not admissible in court and are notoriously unreliable, but they carry weight with the public, and Janus felt that he needed to avoid any discussion in open court of the failed test lest the jury somehow hear of it. Thus his only option was to confront the confessions and seek to convince the jury that the confessions were the unreliable results of Beverly's stress and Riley's manipulations.

Beverly's trial began on October 26 and concluded on November 2, 1992, barely eight months after Burde's death. Beyond the confessions, Jack Lewis and co-counsel Warren Von Schuch presented the forensics, attested to by Dr. Fierro herself; the alleged circumstances of the pregnant Krystyna Drewnowska's supplanting Beverly in Burde's life; an unsigned draft of a new will in which Beverly's share of Burde's estate dropped from a high six figures to a modest five figures; and Zelma Smith. Smith, awaiting sentencing for check fraud and bail jumping, the most recent offenses in a significant criminal career, had contacted Lewis from jail, offering the story that in 1991, a woman whom she now recognized from news accounts to be Beverly had contacted her under an assumed name to try to buy a gun, had even given her several hundred dollars towards expenses. Lewis theorized that Smith provided evidence of premeditation, evidence that Beverly had long considered killing Burde. After the trial, a judge reduced Smith's prison time from seven years to four. Von Schuch offered to the judge on the record, "I think it's a situation where she's entitled to some relief. The commonwealth looks at it as the cost of doing business."

For the defense, Janus offered his own forensics expert who presented a suicide scenario, with Beverly's testimony claiming that Riley tricked her into believing that she was present at Burde's death when she was not, and alibi evidence. Gavin testified about Beverly's 10 P.M. arrival at the house; in summation the prosecutor ridiculed his claim with the sarcastic compliment that Gavin showed loyalty by lying for his mother. Yet Beverly also had a grocery store receipt, and a customer remembered speaking to her in line, which bolstered her alibi.

The jury took only two hours to convict and to agree on a sentence of twenty years. Two jurors later revealed similar accounts of the deliberations. The jurors tried to reenact the shooting and decided that suicide was too awkward. So having decided that Burde had been murdered and having the confessions, the jury convicted Beverly.

For the first round of appeals in the state courts, the Monroes hired Peter Greenspun, and in December 1994, two years after the trial, the Court of Appeals heard oral arguments but eventually ruled in favor of the Commonwealth, as did the state Supreme Court the following year.

Katie Monroe took over researching the case for the approach to federal court. Katie attended conferences where she met experts—among them Richard Leo, who later testified for Beverly—who urged her to pursue Guns Shot Residue (GSR) evidence. For the habeas corpus appeals, Katie had to find constitutional violations, and she focused on the circumstances of the confessions as violative of Beverly's rights and on the hiding of possibly exculpatory evidence, a serious federal violation. The GSR test seemed fertile here, as the expert pointed out that the test existed before trial but had been used neither by Dr. Fierro nor the defense specialist in formulating their theories. By bizarre chance, Beverly herself discovered another instance. Before she went to prison, she met a traveling salesman who used to work at Windsor. He said that he had seen a Chevy Blazer pull out of Windsor on the night of Burde's death, had told police, and had always wondered why he had not been called to testify.

Katie needed official legal help, as she was not a member of the Virginia bar and thus lacked standing to do filings. She convinced Donald Lee to help her. Lee had just joined a Richmond firm after a long stint with the organization that arranged for attorneys for inmates awaiting execution. He knew what habeas petitions would involve. He recruited Stephen Northup, who had worked on capital cases, from another Richmond firm. These men coached Katie through the writing of the petitions and agreed to do the oral arguments.

In federal District Court, Judge Richard L. Williams, who years later would vacate the conviction of Derek Tice, one of the Norfolk Four, asked from the bench how the GSR tests would have changed the way evidence was presented at trial; he even asked the Commonwealth's attorney how to incorporate the evidence into the prosecution's theory. He soon wrote that the claims of ineffective counsel and the Commonwealth's failure to disclose evidence, especially information about Zelma Smith, deserved exploration and merited discovery: that is, he allowed Beverly's side to take depositions from witnesses.

Donald Lee was suffering from cancer during the case, which brought delays to the depositions, so Judge Williams eventually designated the matter to magistrate judge David G. Lowe.

Judge Lowe held a full hearing in December 2000 with live witnesses, including Riley, the prosecutor, and Murray Janus, who explained his failure to object to the confessions. In his April 2001 report, Judge Lowe ruled in the Commonwealth's favor. Stephen Northup, however, found a means of entry for appeal. Both from the bench and in his report, Judge Lowe had decided that Burde had been murdered. He wrote, "Despite Petitioner's protestations to the contrary, the forensic evidence rather conclusively establishes the shot that killed Burde was fired through the fourth and fifth fingers of his right hand as he was holding his head with his hand, probably while asleep." Northup realized that this "finding of fact" was outside the scope of the hearing; by stating it so baldly and perhaps letting it color his view of other evidence, Judge Lowe gave the group grounds for appeal.

Regarding this greatly disputed evidence, after the hearing, another forensics expert concluded that by holding the gun upside down with his left hand and by steadying it with his right, that the position was comfortable and would explain the staining of the fingers. He concluded that Burde shot himself. These battles of experts and experiments render the exact way that Burde died ultimately unknowable.

By the rules of District Court, Judge Williams had to review Judge Lowe's report in any event. He accepted Northup's new brief and held a hearing on September 17, 2001.

On March 28, 2002, Judge Williams vacated the conviction of Beverly Monroe and ordered her freed from prison. Unlike in the Tice case, Judge Williams did not find the confessions to have been obtained illegally. Whereas Tice had asked for a lawyer, Beverly had knowingly waived her rights. Judge Williams wrote, "The Court finds that the tactics engaged in by Riley were deceitful, manipulative, and inappropriate. However, the Court cannot find that his tactics were, in this case, unlawful or unconstitutional." Judge Williams also ruled that Janus's failure to challenge the confessions was a "well-reasoned choice" rather than ineffective counsel.

However, applying *Brady v. Maryland* (1963), which holds that the state must reveal exculpatory evidence, Judge Williams discussed instances in which such evidence remained hidden until exposed during the appeal. The Commonwealth did not reveal its relationship with Zelma Smith and allowed her false claims of her education and employment to be unchallenged at trial. The Commonwealth did not turn over the names of the man who saw the Chevy Blazer. The Commonwealth did not disclose the notes of the secretaries who witnessed Beverly's questioning. (Judge Williams quoted extensively from these notes.) The Commonwealth held back statements from Corinna and from Burde's secretary that Burde was depressed. "Given the net effect of all that was not disclosed," the judge wrote, "there is a reasonable probability that the result would have been different." Finally, Judge Williams said of the forensics, "The physical evidence necessary to show whether Burde's death was a murder or a suicide was, as petitioner argued, either tainted or lost. The forensic evidence presented by the prosecution at trial was unclear and contradictory."

The Commonwealth appealed, but neither the Circuit Court nor the Supreme Court would reverse Judge Williams. With the conviction vacated, the case reverted to being open and Beverly could have faced trial again. In July 2003, the prosecutor for Powhatan County decided not to retry Beverly.

These cases offer several sobering lessons.

These cases very sadly discourage citizens from trusting the police. Indeed, the cases suggest that citizens should not agree to go with police to headquarters, should not agree to interviews, should never waive their rights. And should resist even taking polygraph tests.

Yet all parties should assent that trust between police and citizens is vital. These cases should not reflect on the majority of police who became officers to serve their communities and to be agents for good.

Sherlock Holmes famously told his sidekick Dr. Watson in "A Scandal in Bohemia," "It is a capital mistake to theorize before one has data. Insensibly, one begins to twist facts to suit theories, instead of theories to suit facts." In these cases, the investigators acted from theories formed before they had all the facts. Many famous cases in many other jurisdictions involve officers who waited for analysis of evidence not only before making arrests, but even before interviewing possible suspects.

Investigators must be led by the physical evidence in forming their theories, not by impressions or early reactions. To accuse a person of committing a crime, even during an interview at headquarters, should be done only with sufficient evidentiary foundation.

These cases relied upon disputed confessions, so the fourth lesson is that authorities should conduct questioning in ways to forestall disputes—by taping the entire interview. Beverly Monroe and the Norfolk Four experienced hours of questioning before the police turned on tape recorders. In the twenty-first century, many jurisdictions, now including Norfolk, routinely tape interrogations.

Finally, the cases teach that confessions cannot be accepted simply because they exist. Authorities are obligated to test confessions against the physical and scientific evidence.

CHAPTER 9
The Shootings at Virginia Tech, 2007

At 7:20 A.M. on Monday, April 16, 2007, Virginia Tech police received a call from West Ambler Johnson residence hall. Students had heard a noise from a nearby room and reported that a student might have fallen from a loft bed—a not unusual occurrence.

At 7:24 A.M.—the swift response time merits notice—an officer arrived to discover not an accident but a shooting. Two students, male and female, lay bleeding inside room 4040. More police and rescue personnel were summoned. Within the hour, Virginia Tech police chief Wendell Flinchum and Blacksburg city police chief Kim Crannis arrived at the scene, signaling the importance of the events.

One of the residents of 4040, Heather Hough, arrived at 8:14 to get her roommate for class. The roommate, first-year student Emily Hilscher, had entered the building at 7:02 A.M., according to her access card, which was needed to enter West Ambler before 10 A.M. Emily was one of the shooting victims. Still alive when police first arrived, Emily received medical treatment at two hospitals but expired from her injuries. The male victim, Ryan Christopher Clark, served as the floor's resident advisor and lived in the next room.

Medical workers could not resuscitate him. A triple major in psychology, biology, and English, Clark also played in the Tech marching band.

A man and a woman had been shot in the woman's room; to police, the event looked specific to these people. Hough volunteered that Emily had been with her boyfriend, Karl Thornhill, a student at nearby Radford University. Heather continued that Thornhill often dropped off Emily on Monday mornings, and that Thornhill owned guns. Police quickly declared Thornhill to be a "person of interest," an ominous term that police apply to a potential suspect. Police issued a bulletin for his pickup truck.

At 8:11 A.M., Tech's Chief Flinchum spoke to the school's president, Charles Steger. An alumnus who held three degrees in architecture from Tech, Steger decided to convene the Policy Group, which consisted of the highest-ranking officials at the school. As they gathered, three Policy Group members leaked word of the shootings to family members or associates. One sent an e-mail message to Richmond: "Gunman on the loose . . . This is not releasable yet . . . just try to make sure it doesn't get out." At 8:40, Flinchum informed Steger by phone that police sought "a person of interest." At this time, the event seemed specific and isolated.

Regarding Thornhill, the official report of the events at Tech includes this understated line, "the police agencies involved in stopping and questioning [him] did not treat him sympathetically; he deserved better care." At 9:24, a county sheriff's deputy stopped Thornhill's truck and detained him. After 9:30, a state trooper arrived and performed a gunshot test on Thornhill's hands, then preserved the test for later analysis. But the encounter satisfied these officers of Thornhill's innocence, and they passed that opinion on and it got to the Policy Group. As the group dealt with this new dilemma, at 9:48 the police with Thornhill received calls about shootings at Tech's Norris Hall and quickly left for the scene.

But the police were not done with Thornhill. That night, with a search warrant, they entered his apartment, handcuffed him and his family members, and forced them to the floor. Police still suspected that the shootings in West Ambler could be unrelated to the shootings in Norris. Only when ballistics experts matched the bullets from both shootings was Thornhill cleared of suspicion.

This chapter relies on several journalistic pieces and three key in-depth accounts. First is *April 16th: Virginia Tech Remembers* edited by Roger Lazenby. A journalism professor at Tech, Lazenby was conducting a class in a different building when shooting began in Norris Hall. He put his class to work getting information and posting it on the student journalism website. The book gathers these early reports and extensive statements from students and faculty directly involved. Next is *No Right to Remain Silent* by Lucinda Roy, who was chair of English at Tech. Her book provides a faculty perspective and acts as a counterpoint to the third source, *Mass Shootings at Virginia Tech: Report of the Review Panel*, hereafter referred to as the "Panel Report." Gov. Timothy M. Kaine convened a panel to study the events and report its findings, which it did in August 2007, and again with an addendum in November 2009. The Panel Report provides the minute-by-minute account of the day; the following narrative uses the amended timeline from the 2009 addendum.

Police locked down West Ambler to allow for interviews of residents. They lifted the blockade to allow students to get to 9:05 classes. Two students then went to Norris Hall, where they died.

The Policy Group debated from 8:25 through 9:30 on what the university should do regarding the shootings. At least two aspects impacted their deliberations. One was logistics: they were not sure that a campus of 2,600 acres with 26,000 students could be locked down. The Panel Report includes these observations: "When a murder takes place in a city of 35,000 population [number of students plus staff at Tech], the entire city is virtually never shut down. At most, some in the vicinity of the shooting might be alerted if it is thought that the shooter is in the neighborhood. . . A university, how-ever, in some ways has more control than does the mayor or police of a city . . . The university is also considered by many to be playing a role in *loco parentis*."

The other aspect was the incident involving William Morva. In August 2006, Morva, an escaped convict, shot three people, two fatally, over two days. The deaths occurred near Tech, so the administration closed the school. A mother of an employee misunderstood her daughter's call and alerted police to a hostage situation. A SWAT team charged a building to discover no such problems inside. This overreaction may have discouraged officials from issuing a broad announcement about the shootings in West Ambler. (Morva was apprehended away from Tech's grounds.) At 9:26 the school sent this e-mail alert to the community: "A shooting incident occurred at West Ambler Johnson earlier this morning. Police are on the scene and are investigating. The university community is urged to be cautious." The Panel Report later judged that the message should have been sent sooner and should have admitted that homicides had occurred.

Before April 16, 2007, few universities would have gone into lockdown due to a violent incident at a residence hall located away from the central grounds. After that day, most universities would go into full alert mode in such circumstances.

The decision not to lock down the school became problematic as soon as it was made, as police then informed the Policy Group at about 9:30 that Thornhill was an unlikely suspect. So the shooter could be anywhere. As they mulled over this information, at 9:45, President Steger, who could see Norris Hall from the window, heard gunshots and saw police charging the building.

While administrators debated and police sought Thornhill, English major Seung Hui Cho, age twenty-three, prepared himself for his demise. His entry card records that he entered his residence hall at 7:17 A.M. He left bloodstained clothing in his room. At 7:25, he deleted his e-mail account and online files. He disposed of his computer's hard drive and cell phone; they were never recovered. At 9:01, according to the postmarks, he mailed a package to NBC News in New York; people saw him at the post office. At the same time, he sent a letter to the Department of English, complaining about Professor Carl Bean.

Norris Hall

A large building typical of university architecture, Norris Hall bears the name of a longtime dean of engineering. Though it was the home of the Department of Engineering Science and Mechanics and faculty laboratories, Norris provided classrooms for many subjects. On the third floor that morning, a large class was taking an accounting exam. On the second floor, where the shootings occurred, classes in engineering, French, and German were going on.

The attacks involved five classrooms on the second floor. The first calls to 911, from students in the rooms, came in at 9:41 A.M.

An Asian-looking man with short hair opened doors and looked into several of the classrooms. Then he returned.

The attacker began with room 206, a graduate engineering class. He shot and killed the professor and nine of the thirteen students. Perhaps because real gunfire does not sound like TV and movie gunfire, students from nearby classes thought the noises were from construction, and one class went on with the day's lesson. The killer then burst into the German class in room 207, shot the professor dead, and shot eleven of the twelve students, four of them fatally. Survivor Derek O'Dell recalls the shooter: "He was very calm, very determined, methodical in his killing. He shot as he opened the door. He was going along the front row shooting people." The killer never spoke, and showed only a blank expression. He used two handguns, a 9mm Glock and a .22-caliber Walther. When the shooter left the room, O'Dell and Katelyn Carney rushed to the front, shut the door, and braced it with their legs. Others joined them, and O'Dell realized that he was bleeding.

In room 205, a computer course, students realized what was happening and blockaded the door with the teacher's desk. The killer tried to push his way in, but students put pressure on the desk to keep the door shut. The killer shot through the door, then moved on. In room 211, a French course, the killer murdered the professor and eleven students, injuring six others. The killer returned to 207, but could not get through the door. He shot through the door, resumed his attack in 211, then moved on.

In room 204, engineering professor Liviu Librescu, a Holocaust survivor in his 'seventies, blocked the door with his body while students fled through the windows. Unlike the other rooms, the windows here dropped nineteen feet onto bushes and grass, so students could jump. The killer shot through the door and gained entry. He shot the professor at close range and fired at students still in the room, killing one. He tried a third time to enter 207; when he could not, he surveyed his work in 206 and 211. At some point, a professor, Kevin Granata, came down from the third floor to investigate and was killed.

In Norris, thirty people had been shot to death and seventeen wounded.

Police assaulted the building at 9:45, less than four minutes after the first call. In 1999, during the shootings at Columbine High School in Colorado, police delayed entering the school to engage the shooters; the Virginia police exhibited no timidity. But they found the three main doors chained shut from the inside. Police tried to shoot open the doors, to no avail. Finally, they shot the lock at the unchained machine shop door and gained entrance.

As police came into the building, the killer committed suicide with one of his guns. His body fell in room 211, among the French class. He had fired 174 rounds, and he had 203 remaining. Police soon identified him as Seung Hui Cho. His guns had been used that morning at West Ambler.

At 9:50, this e-mail message went out to the Tech community: "A gunman is loose on the campus. Stay in buildings until further notice. Stay away from all windows."

While in lockdown with his class, journalism professor Roger Lazenby thought, "After the August shootings and lockdown [the Morva incident] I had been disappointed that I hadn't pushed my students to begin reporting on the incident. I decided on this morning that I wasn't going to have more regrets about inaction. The Virginia Tech community needed information, and we were going to provide it." Using sources that young people know, such as Facebook, the students gathered information, verified it, prepared copy, and posted it on the journalism website, planetblacksburg.com. The student newspaper also went into action on its site. Many national news organizations linked to these sites as the most immediate sources of information.

The Hokies

Early in new millennium, speaking before a gathering of alumni, a high-ranking athletic administrator from the University of Virginia had joked about Tech's joining UVA in the Atlantic Coast Conference, "Sometimes I think that if we have to go Blacksburg [for games], everybody else should too."

Indeed, UVA can and does boast of its colorful location and its proximity to Washington and Richmond. In contrast, Tech sits deep in the Appalachian Mountains in the southwest sector of the state, over 230 miles from Washington. In 1872, the Virginia legislature chose Blacksburg as the site for its land grant college because a school already existed there, the Preston and Olin Institute, a tiny place run by Methodists. With funds provided by the federal government in accordance with the Morrill Land-Grant College Act, the Commonwealth purchased a building and a small parcel from the Institute, then purchased a tract for use as a farm. Thus was founded the Virginia Agricultural and Mechanical College.

From its inception, two factors helped to mold and to unify the school—its isolation in a rural community far from Virginia's cities and its rivalry with its famous, academically innovative, and somewhat pretentious neighbor to the north, UVA. In 1896, the school added "Polytechnic Institute" to its name, and in 1970 was renamed "Virginia Polytechnic Institute and State University." The school had sought to become Virginia State, a name that would place it with America's major state schools, such as Penn State, but another college already claimed that name. Through much of the twentieth century the school was known as "VPI," but by the 1980s the appellation "Virginia Tech" had become popular and preferred. Through vigorous marketing, enhanced academic departments, and successful athletic teams (well, mainly football teams), Virginia Tech became a national brand. Its entry into the ACC in 2004 cemented its status, worthy of being listed with Georgia Tech, the University of Maryland, Duke University, and UVA.

As Tech unofficially shed the name VPI, it also shed its athletic nickname, the Gobblers. As early as 1896, Tech fans yelled a nonsense phrase that began "Hoki! Hoki! Hoki Hy! Tech!" An "e" somehow appended itself to the first word, and the Tech teams were the Hokies. Nobody knows what a Hokie is, a situation similar to that with UVA's Wahoos and Georgetown University's Hoyas. The odd sound and the obscure origin are parts of the nickname's charm. And "Hokies" does seem preferable to "Gobblers."

America's major universities—Harvard, Michigan, UVA, and so on—maintain their lofty status by making students proud to attend them. Something about the atmospheres of these schools inspires and unifies students. The aftermath of the shootings displayed such spirit at Tech.

At the memorial service held on April 17, less than a day and a half after the shootings, Governor Kaine spoke of being in Japan when he learned of the crisis and of his ten-hour wait to return to Virginia. During the wait, he watched news accounts, and he told the thousands at the service in the arena and the thousands more watching at the football stadium how much he admired the students who spoke to the reporters.

> What the students came back to, wearing the Virginia Tech sweatshirts, wearing the Virginia Tech hats, was the incredible community spirit, and the sense of unity here on this campus. . . in the darkest moment in the history of this university, the world saw you and saw you respond in a way that built community.

Poet and English Professor Nikki Giovanni, an ironic choice to speak given her encounters with Cho (as will be discussed below), added to the Governor's remarks with her prose poem written for the event.

> We are Virginia Tech. . . We are strong enough to stand tall fearlessly, we are brave enough to bend to cry, and we are sad enough to know that we must laugh again. . . We are Virginia Tech. . . we are better than we think we are and not quite what we want to be. . . We will continue to invent the future through our blood and tears and through all our sadness . . . We are the Hokies. . . We will prevail.

As she flamboyantly stepped back from the podium, the crowd erupted into the sustained chant, "Let's Go Hokies!" Student reporter Kevin Cupp wrote of the poem and the chant, "it was just such an overwhelming change of mood and sense of Hokie spirit. With that kind of spirit, we can get through anything."

This spirit also showed itself in how the Hokies reacted to Cho's family, according to Lazenby. On the Drillfield, a campus landmark, mourners placed thirty-three Hokie stones—large local rocks—to mourn the dead. Significantly, the number was thirty-three, including Cho, not thirty-two, and few efforts arose to remove the thirty-third. In contrast, Dave Cullen reports in his book *Columbine* that after the killings at Columbine in 1999, a mourner planted makeshift crosses for all the dead, including for the two killers; family members of victims destroyed those two crosses. (Lucinda Roy dissents from this view; she writes that Cho's stone kept being removed and then replaced, to be removed again.) Cullen reports on the vilification of the parents of both Columbine shooters. Again in contrast, the *Washington Post* reported in 2008, "The FBI helped to deliver to Cho's family hundreds of letters and other items left at Virginia Tech . . . Some of the letters contained threats, blaming them for what happened. But most were filled with prayers and words of comfort and sympathy, assuring them that what their son did was not their fault."

Cho's parents wisely sought out an attorney to speak for them, and wisely chose Wade Smith, one of the preeminent attorneys in North Carolina. He gained wide fame for his representation of the interests of Bonnie Von Stein after her husband was murdered, allegedly by her son's friends, in a case reported by Joe McGinniss in *Cruel Doubt* (1991). In 2006-07, Smith was one of the lead defense attorneys in the Duke lacrosse case. On April 20, Smith issued a statement, credited to Cho's sister Sun Kyung, a Princeton graduate who worked as a contractor in the State Department.

> On behalf of our family, we are so deeply sorry for the devastation my brother has caused. . . We are humbled by this darkness. We feel hopeless, helpless and lost. This was someone that I grew up with and loved. Now I feel like I didn't know this person. . . He has made the world weep.

Cho's parents went into seclusion, refusing all media contacts and even declining to take calls from relatives and friends. On the first anniversary of the shootings, Wade Smith echoed Sun Kyung's statement as he told the *Post* of Cho's parents, "They continue to live in darkness."

Seung Hui Cho

At Tech, Cho lived a reclusive life. His suitemates barely knew him; they claimed that he resisted their overtures to become friends. He was silent in class. He often wore a baseball cap and dark glasses, creating a distancing demeanor that annoyed people, including professors Roy and Giovanni, who both asked him to remove the glasses. His contributions in creative writing classes tended to have violent plotlines. He received reprimands for harassment of two women.

On the surface these aspects are not that ominous. College-age guys have worn caps and shades for decades and enjoy that these accessories sometimes annoy authority figures. Violent stories are staples in creative writing classes, and professors usually know how to handle such submissions. And plenty of young men need to learn the proper boundaries in how to approach women. Yet with Cho, these aspects, which would be learning experiences or habits to be outgrown with most young men, presaged great turmoil.

Cho's parents tried to help him adjust. Sung Tae Cho and Hyang Im Cho came to America from Korea in 1992 seeking what immigrants always seek—a better life for the next generation. With their daughter they fulfilled the American Dream. But Seung Hui plunged them into darkness.

Born in 1984, Cho endured severe childhood illnesses that exacerbated his quiet nature. He recoiled from contact, especially verbal but also physical. The family eventually bought a townhouse in Centreville, Virginia, and Mr. Cho worked many hours as a dry cleaner. Mrs. Cho also worked long hours outside the home. Increasingly concerned about their son's refusal to socialize and even to speak, the Chos sought counseling when Seung entered middle school. His psychiatrist diagnosed social anxiety disorder with selective mutism, a refusal to speak. Cho attended therapy and took an antidepressant drug. At Westfield High School, Cho received special accommodations that excused him from class discussions and limited oral performance to short sessions with teachers. A steady worker with good intelligence, Cho took honors courses and graduated with a fine GPA of 3.52.

Cho chose Tech, though high school counselors urged him and his family to consider a small college close to home. With tight supervision, regular therapy, adjusted assignments, and family support, Cho had negotiated high school. None of these aids would be available at Tech. But he insisted on going there. To ease the transition, his parents visited him every Sunday during his first semester. They took as a hopeful sign of assertiveness his request for a room change: Cho, extremely neat and orderly, could not abide his messy roommate. After this first semester, his parents talked to him by phone each Sunday, including April 15, 2007.

Cho started at Tech in 2003, and for three of his four years there he lived in residence halls. In his second year, he lived off-site with a senior whose work schedule kept him away most of the time. All Cho's suitemates and roommates told similar stories about him. If they tried to talk him, he would ignore them or give single-word replies. If they took him to the dining hall with them, he never took part in conversations. One group dragged him to a party where he took out a knife and stabbed the rug. They ceased trying to draw him out and merely coexisted.

He started at Tech as a business information systems major— working with computers seemed to fit his withdrawn state. But he changed to English. His choice of English and his choice to concentrate on creative writing, with small classes that demanded self-expression and participation, make no psychological sense and constitute a great mystery of his life. An influence may have been a large lecture class on poetry that he took during spring 2004, taught by novelist and poet Lucinda Roy, who was also the chair of the department. Later that fall, she received an e-mail message from him asking advice about getting a short novel published. She answered with the expected cautions: Getting an agent is very difficult, he should read books on getting agents, he should take creative writing courses.

Cho described his manuscript this way: "sort of like Tom Sawyer except that it's a bit silly in a lot of ways . . . I don't know if there's a market or audience for my writing because it's really silly and pathetic depending on how you look at it, but that's what I'm trying to find out." The tone here, self-deprecating and timid, contrasts with the anger of the coming years. During late spring 2005, his sister found a rejection letter from a New York publisher among Cho's papers. She tried to be encouraging, though he would not let her read his work. Perhaps willing to soldier on with writing even after this rejection, Cho registered for creative writing classes.

In fall 2005, Cho experienced troubles in class, troubles with women, and troubles with his sanity. In creative writing class, Nikki Giovanni, who would lift the spirits of Tech after the shootings, could not tolerate Cho's reflector glasses and hat and demanded that he remove them. Cho took cell phone pictures of students during class; classmates were uncomfortable around him. He resisted reading his work aloud. Indeed, the regular oral critiques and discussions that comprise such classes would seem to be profound obstacles for a man with an anxiety disorder. The students one day went on a tangent about eating meat; Cho responded in a following session with a composition, read aloud, expressing his disgust for the students as a bunch of "low-life barbarians," "despicable human beings," and "cannibals." Giovanni would take no more. In mid October, she told Roy that she wanted Cho removed from the course.

After reading Cho's piece, Roy e-mailed four units at Tech: Student Affairs, the Counseling Center, the Liberal Arts college's main office, and the Tech police. After meeting with Cho, wisely choosing to have another professor present as a witness, Roy became convinced that he needed counseling and openly urged him to request it.

Cho protested to Roy that his piece was a satire, in the mode of Jonathan Swift's "A Modest Proposal," and that he did not want to lose the credits for the course. He agreed to finish the course as an independent study with Roy and another professor, though Roy mostly met with him. For the remainder of the semester, they discussed poems by William Butler Yeats and Emily Dickinson and worked on his own poetry. She assigned him a grade of A. Yet she also relentlessly urged him to seek counseling. She called the Counseling Center and harangued them to come to her office to meet with him and see his condition; the reply was that by policy, they could only meet with students who came to them.

In late fall 2005, as Cho finished work for Lucinda Roy, he engaged in awkward and disturbing approaches to female students. Twice Tech police visited him, on November 27 and December 13. The women alleged that Cho sent text messages and Facebook postings that were not threatening but odd. He wrote lines from Shakespeare's *Romeo and Juliet* on the message board at the second woman's room. Police told him not to approach the women again in any way. Neither woman took the matter into the Judicial Affairs system. A flurry of e-mail messages confirms that Residence Life officials knew about the second incident.

After police left Cho on December 13, he sent an instant message to a suitemate: "I might as well kill myself now." Alarmed, the student summoned police, who returned and took Cho into custody. A magistrate allowed Cho to be held overnight at a psychiatric hospital. This "involuntary commitment" became important in the later matter of the gun purchases. On the following day, a psychologist, a psychiatrist, and then a hearing officer all found Cho not to be a danger to self or others; the hearing officer ordered outpatient treatment. Records from the hospital arrived via fax at Tech's Counseling Center, and Cho met with staff on the afternoon of his release. He did not meet with them again. Because Cho was an adult, Tech officials did not notify his parents of these events.

These episodes indicate that several administrators at Tech knew that Cho exhibited troubling behaviors: the people that Lucinda Roy warned, Roy herself, the Tech police, the RA administrators, the Counseling Center. No system centralized all this information. In combination, these troubles could convince that Cho needed an intervention, but no one saw the entire combination. And the units tended to cite privacy laws as reasons not to contact other units. The Panel Report refers to this situation: "Privacy laws can block some

attempts to share information, but even more often may cause hold-
ers of such information to default to the non-disclosure option—
even when laws permit the option to disclose." Cho's parents later
told the panel that had they known of his behaviors that they would
have pulled him from school and sought help. Indeed, their history
shows that they got their son help when he needed it.

The year 2006 was uneventful for Cho, as far as is known. At
home he remained quiet; he did not work during vacations. Cho
continued taking writing classes, writing more violent stories in a
Fiction Workshop and earning only a D-plus; in another Fiction
Writing class he managed a B-plus. Technical Writing with Carl
Bean proved too great a challenge. Cho would not work in groups,
wrote research on an unapproved topic, and dropped the class after
yelling at Bean. The letter about Bean that Cho mailed on April 16,
2007, likely stems from this altercation.

Starting in early February 2007, credit card purchases show Cho
was procuring guns and bullets. He bought the Walther first, order-
ing it online and retrieving it at a pawn shop. More than thirty days
later, in keeping with Virginia's one-gun-purchase-per-month law,
he bought the Glock at Roanoke Firearms. He bought the ammuni-
tion in small amounts from eBay, Wal-Mart, and Dick's Sporting
Goods. His buying pattern intelligently avoided a massive purchase
that would raise suspicions.

Investigators could not link Cho to Emily Hilscher, who was
shot a West Ambler. A witness saw Cho in the mailroom of West
Ambler before 7 A.M.; he had entry-card access to this room, but not
to other areas. Emily entered at 7:02, according to her card. The
panel theorized that he followed her when she entered the building,
a sad coincidence. The theory continues that RA Clark heard noises
in 4040, went to assist Emily, and was shot. Why the attacks started
with a random person in a residence hall, two hours before the
shootings at Norris, defies explanation. The selection of Norris
explains itself more readily: The killer probably wanted a building
known to house occupied classrooms.

The Columbine shooters left videotaped statements in their
homes. The police seized the tapes and released them to select media

in very small bits; the entire tapes were never widely shown. Cho, who according to teachers had been obsessed with Columbine when it occurred in 1999, circumvented the police by sending his statement directly to the media. The package to NBC News, mailed at 9:01 on April 16, included an 1,800-word written rant along with a DVD of scenes and images of Cho posing with guns and reading an angry statement. NBC never released the full contents, but did broadcast significant sections. Speaking to the camera, Cho refers to the Columbine shooters as the "martyrs like Eric and Dylan." He says:

> You had a hundred billion chances and ways to have avoided today
> . . . But you decided to spill my blood. You forced me into a corner
> and you gave me only one option. The decision was yours. Now
> you have blood on your hands that will never wash off. . .Did you
> want to inject as much misery into our lives as you can just because
> you can? . . .
>
> You had everything you wanted. Your Mercedes wasn't enough,
> you brats. Your golden necklaces weren't enough, you snobs. Your
> trust fund wasn't enough. Your vodka and Cognac weren't enough.
> All your debaucheries weren't enough. Those weren't enough to
> fulfill your hedonistic needs. You had everything.

That Cho refers to himself as representative of an oppressed group is an ironic claim coming from a loner. The verbal assault does not specify anyone by name. Cho was taking a course on the Bible as literature, which might account for the biblical, prophet-like cadences in the last section quoted above.

Contexts

Individuals in ancient and medieval times may have wanted to commit mass murder, but they lacked the technology (unless they commanded an army). The twentieth century provided the means. In 1927, in Bath, Michigan, fifty-five-year-old farmer and school board member Andrew Kehoe distributed explosives and timers throughout a grade school. Not all the timers worked, but those that did caused massive destruction. Kehoe, facing financial problems and blaming tax increases, had burned his farm and killed himself by exploding his shrapnel-filled car. The dead numbered forty-five, thirty-eight of them children ages seven to twelve.

Another early instance of mass murder is the spree by Howard Unruh, a World War II veteran who on September 6, 1949, walked along the streets of Camden, New Jersey, shooting and killing thirteen people. Courts declared him criminally insane.

List-makers of attacks on schools tend to start not with Kehoe but with either of two more recent shooters. In 1966, Charles Whitman, age twenty-five, killed fourteen people by gunfire at the Tower at the University of Texas in Austin. In 1979, California teenager Brenda Ann Spencer shot at an elementary school across from her home, killing two adults and wounding eight children. The Panel Report includes a list of forty school shootings from 1979 through 2007. The list in a study by Marcel Lebrun includes over seventy school shootings for the same period. Not all of those on either list quite match Cho or Whitman or Spencer; some are clearly workplace shootings or killings involving domestic situations. And the lists could expand if they included people such as Howard Unruh or Sylvia Seegrist, who shot people at a Pennsylvania shopping mall in 1985—that is, shooters whose goal was mass murder at a communal setting.

A broad analysis may place Cho not only in the context of Columbine shooters Eric Harris and Dylan Klebold, but also in the context of Unruh, Whitman, and Seegrist. In these instances, Cho included, individuals with generalized anger sought to express that rage through a spree killing. They selected settings that they knew, where they felt confident, and where they would find large numbers of people, such as a school, a mall, a city street, or a restaurant. The wide availability of a weapon that can be used to kill many people in a short time span has surely been a factor in the increasing number of such attacks.

The Issues Raised

Three days after the shootings, Governor Kaine established a panel to review the events, to create an accurate account of what occurred, and to propose needed reforms. The panel consisted of eight members, chaired by a retired Virginia State Police superintendent and including Tom Ridge, the first U.S. Secretary of Homeland Security. Lucinda Roy perceptively notes that only two of the eight came from colleges, and those two from medical schools; that is, no one on the panel taught undergraduates or was familiar with the current undergraduate college experience.

The Panel Report, issued in August 2007 and reissued with addenda in November 2009, closes most chapters with a list of recommendations. These recommendations number more than seventy. The following paragraphs examine broad themes in the Panel Report and other sources.

Lockdown in Response to Crisis. Tech's Policy Group opted, on the morning of April 16, for wide notification via e-mail of the shootings in West Ambler. Having such an e-mail notification system in place put Tech ahead of many other colleges. The shootings convinced schools around the country to adopt such notification systems and to develop emergency protocols.

While the Policy Group debated closing the school on that morning, other institutions acted more decisively upon hearing the police reports about the shootings in West Ambler. The superintendent of the Blacksburg public schools put them in lockdown at 8:52 A.M. As early as 8:25 Tech's police canceled the regular bank deposit retrievals—but the reason could be that police needed all available hands. Tech's Professional and Continuing Education Center and Tech's veterinary college locked down on their own initiatives, the former at 8 A.M. And, embarrassingly, three administrators sent word to outsiders about the shootings. The Panel Report wonders if a total lockdown, ordered very early, would have deterred the attacks at Norris. The package to NBC constituted a confession in advance, but Cho had not mailed it until 9:01. The decision not to close the school, as rational and explainable as it may have been, haunts discussion of that day.

Records and Privacy. Administrators across the nation cite two federal laws that guarantee the privacy rights of individuals: HIPAA, which concerns electronic health records, and FERPA, which concerns educational records. Records need the assent of their subject to be shared (if the subject is an adult). Administrators, often fearful of lawsuits, opt for nondisclosure of records to others in almost all instances. In simplest terms, policies to protect privacy prevented units at Tech from exchanging information about Cho and from notifying his parents. Media reports tended to adopt Lucinda Roy as a hero in the story because she agitated, to no avail, for some agency to intervene in Cho's troubled life. The Panel Report concludes that, "The problems presented by a seriously troubled student often require a group effort. The current state of information privacy law and practice is inadequate to accomplish this task."

Guns. The shortest chapter in the Panel Report, a mere six pages, addresses the matter of Cho's weapons, the guns. Virginia has long been friendly to gun ownership, and the legislature has resisted efforts to curtail rights of ownership and purchase. Virginia's one-gun-purchase-per-month law, which Cho obeyed, is thus somewhat remarkable.

The Panel Report bluntly states that having been judged, even temporarily, as a danger to himself on that night in December 2005, that Cho was ineligible to buy a gun under federal law. Virginia's statute seems to focus on "involuntary commitment" as a disqualification, and the Panel Report cannot be definitive whether the state restriction would apply to Cho. But the federal law should have applied, if Virginia authorities had listed him, which they had not. The court did not provide his name for listing.

Cho followed legal procedures with each gun purchase: He filled out two forms, which were transmitted by the dealer to the state police, who checked Cho's name against federal and state databases. Cho's name did not appear; he was not flagged as disqualified due to mental health issues, despite his night in a facility. The probable reason: The outcome of his case was an order for *outpatient* treatment, not *inpatient* treatment, and in Virginia, the latter is the disqualifier. The Panel Report points out this conflict of federal and state laws in how to interpret the mental health disqualification and in how to determine what names get listed.

That the Report's discussion of guns focuses on Cho's qualifications to purchase a gun and not on the ready availability of the guns and the bullets reflects that the events did not shake the Commonwealth's traditional stance regarding gun ownership.

A controversial aspect of Virginia's gun laws is that gun show purchases require no background checks. Though Cho bought his guns at dealers and not at shows, the Tech shootings revived interest in closing this "loophole," as reformers referred to it. Governor Kaine asked the legislature to impose such checks at gun shows, but the bill died in committee in January 2008.

Treatment of Citizens by Police. Only in subtext does the Panel Report address how law enforcement dealt with citizens. As discussed earlier, Karl Thornhill, the boyfriend of the first victim, was treated as a suspect that morning and later handcuffed and forced to the floor while his rooms were searched. That same evening, April 16, authorities burst into Cho's suite and handcuffed suitemates while police conducted a search. (This point appears in Lazenby's book, not the Report.) As police cleared Norris Hall, they pointed guns at the already frightened people and ordered them to walk with hands raised, including the wounded, like Derek O'Dell, who had to hold in his mouth the belt that closed the wound in his arm. (TV shows and movies usually portray this kind of rescue scene as one of relief and embrace between citizens and police; not so in real life, both at Columbine and at Tech.) The Panel Report states, "The police had their priorities straight. Although many survivors were frightened, the police understandably were focused on clearing the building safely and quickly." The Report continues that police had to confirm that there was no second shooter.

Response Times. The Panel Report praises the swift responses to the 911 calls, under five minutes to both West Ambler and Norris. Police shot their way into Norris within five minutes of their arrival.

Settlement. In June 2008, Tech paid out $11 million to twenty-eight families of victims. Two families did not join the suit but filed separate actions, and two families did not sue. The agreement included medical expenses for the injured.

The Return to Norris Hall

As school officials debated over what to do with Norris Hall, the Chair of Engineering Science and Mechanics, Ishwar Puri, advocated that his faculty be allowed to return to their laboratories and continue their research. Though some people wanted the building demolished or gutted, Puri pleaded that the elaborate labs be preserved, adding that ongoing research would be an appropriate way to honor fallen colleagues. At the end of 2007, officials agreed the leave Puri's faculty and labs in the building. The second floor would become a Center for Peace Studies and Violence Prevention.

BIBLIOGRAPHY

The journalistic sources for each case appear in *chronological order*.
Thus by reading the headlines, you can get a chronology of the case.

About the History of Virginia

Dabney, Virgnius. *Virginia: The New Dominion*. Garden City, NY: Doubleday, 1971.

Rubin, Louis D., Jr. *Virginia: A History*. New York: Norton, 1984.

About the History of the South

Carter, Dan T. *Scottsboro: A Tragedy of the American South*. Revised Edition. Baton Rouge: Louisiana State University Press, 1979.

Cooper, William J., Jr., and Thomas E. Terrill. *The American South: A History*. New York: Knopf, 1990.

Craven, Avery O. *The Growth of Southern Nationalism, 1848-1861*. Baton Rouge: Louisiana State University Press, 1953.

Genovese, Eugene D. *Roll, Jordan, Roll: The World the Slaves Made*. New York: Random House, 1974.

Kolchin, Peter. *American Slavery: 1619-1877*. New York: Hill and Wang, 1993.

Woodward, C. Vann. *Origins of the New South*. Baton Rouge: Louisiana State University Press, 1951.

About Nancy Randolph

Adams, William Howard. *Gouverneur Morris: An Independent Life*. New Haven, CT: Yale University Press, 2003.

Baker, Leonard. *John Marshall: A Life in Law*. New York: Macmillan, 1974.

Biddle, Francis. "Scandal at Bizarre." *American Heritage* 12.5 (August 1961): 10-13, 79-82.

Brady, Patricia. Review of *Unwise Passions*, by Alan Pell Crawford. *The Virginia Magazine of History and Biography* 10.3 (2002): 403-404.

Brookhiser, Richard. *Gentleman Revolutionary: Gouverneur Morris—The Rake Who Wrote the Constitution*. New York: Free Press, 2003.

Bruce, William Cabell. *John Randolph of Roanoke*. 2 Vols. New York: Putnam's, 1922.

Crawford, Alan Pell. "A House Called Bizarre." *Washington Post*, November 26, 2000.

————. *Unwise Passions: A True Story of a Remarkable Woman—and the First Great Scandal of Eighteenth-Century America*. New York: Simon and Schuster, 2000.

Daniels, Jonathan. *The Randolphs of Virginia*. Garden City, NY: Doubleday, 1972.

Dawidoff, Robert. *The Education of John Randolph*. New York: Norton, 1979.

Eckenrode, H. J. *The Randolphs: The Story of a Family*. Indianapolis: Bobbs-Merrill, 1946.

Kirschke, James J. *Gouverneur Morris: Author, Statesman, and Man of the World*. New York: St. Martin's, 2005.

Marshall, John. "Commonwealth v. Randolph: Notes on Evidence." In *The Papers of John Marshall*, Vol. 2, edited by Charles T. Cullen and Herbert A. Johnson, 161-178. Chapel Hill: University of North Carolina Press, 1977.

————. "Correspondence with Gouverneur Morris, December 1809." In *The Papers of John Marshall*, Vol. 7, edited by Charles F. Hobson, 219-224. Chapel Hill: University of North Carolina Press, 1993.

Meade, Robert Douthat. *Patrick Henry: Practical Revolutionary*. Philadelphia: Lippincott, 1969.

The Papers of Thomas Jefferson, Vol. 25, edited by John Catanzariti. Princeton, NJ: Princeton University Press, 1992.

About George Wythe

Boyd, Julian P., and W. Edwin Hemphill. *The Murder of George Wythe: Two Essays*. Williamsburg, VA: The Institute for Early American History and Culture, 1955.

Brodie, Fawn. *Thomas Jefferson: An Intimate History*. New York: Norton, 1974.

Brown, Imogene E. *American Aristides: A Biography of George Wythe*. Rutherford, NJ: Fairleigh Dickinson University Press, 1981.

Chadwick, Bruce. *I Am Murdered: George Wythe, Thomas Jefferson, and the Killing That Shocked a New Nation*. Hoboken, NJ: Wiley, 2009

Dill, Alonzo Thomas. *George Wythe: Teacher of Liberty*. Williamsburg: Virginia Independence Bicentennial Commission, 1979.

Jarrett, Calvin. "Was George Wythe Murdered?" *Virginia Cavalcade* (Winter 1963-64).

McLaughlin, Jack, ed. *To His Excellency Thomas Jefferson: Letters to a President*. New York: Norton, 1991.

Munford, George Wythe. *The Two Parsons; Cupid's Sports; The Dream; and the Jewels of Virginia*. Richmond: J. D. K. Sleight, 1884.

About the Martinsville Seven

Kennedy, Randall. *Race, Crime, and the Law*. New York: Random, 1997.
Rise, Eric W. *The Martinsville Seven: Race, Rape, and Capital Punishment*. Charlottesville: University Press of Virginia, 1995.

About Alexandra Bruce

Books

Lankford, Nelson D. *The Last American Aristocrat: The Biography of David K. E. Bruce, 1898-1977*. Boston: Little, Brown, 1996.
Mellen, Joan. *Privilege: The Enigma of Sasha Bruce*. New York: Dial, 1982.

Articles

Kerney, J. Regan, and John Rigos. "Husband of Bruce Daughter Charged: U. S. Extradition of Greek Sought in Bruce Death." *Washington Post*, 25 October 1978.
Kerney, J. Regan. "Mate Denies Killing Bruce's Daughter." *Washington Post*, 26 October 1978.
———. "Officials Seize Items Held by Husband in Bruce Case." *Washington Post*, 27 October 1978.
"A Gothic Romance in Old Virginia." *Time*, 6 November 1978.
Kerney, J. Regan. "Bruce Husband Charged with Murder Sets Conditions for Return to Va. Trial." *Washington Post*, 10 November 1978.
———. "Sasha Bruce: Clouded by Mystery; Sasha Bruce's Life of Isolation Ends in Mysterious Death." *Washington Post*, 14 November 1978.
Zito, Tom. "Gumshoe in His Golden Days: Downey Rice, 65, Is Still on the Case." *Washington Post*, 29 November 1978.
"Downey Rice Dies, Lawyer and Private Investigator." *Washington Post*, 4 December 1978.
McCall, Cheryl. "Heiress Sasha Bruce, Her Husband Is Accused: There the Riddle Begins." *People Weekly*, 18 December 1978.
Lynton, Stephen J. "Probe Drags on into Death of Envoy's Daughter." *Washington Post*, 31 July 1979.
Jacoby, Susan. "Public Service and Private Pain." Review of *Privilege: The Enigma of Sasha Bruce*, by Joan Mellen. *New York Times*, 10 October 1982.
Gamarekian, Barbara. "Diplomat's Widow Aids the Young." *New York Times*, 4 August 1984.
Levy, Claudia. "Evangeline Bell Bruce Dies; Washington Hostess, Author." *Washington Post*, 14 December 1995.
See also: Sasha Bruce Youthwork, *www.sashabruce.org*.

About the Timothy Spencer Case

Books

Douglas, John, and Mark Olshaker. *Journey into Darkness: Follow the FBI's Premier Investigative Profiler as he Penetrates the Minds and Motives of the Most Terrifying Serial Killers*. New York: Scribner, 1997.

Mones, Paul. *Stalking Justice: The Dramatic True Story of the Detective Who First Used DNA Testing to Catch a Serial Killer*. New York: Simon and Schuster, 1995.

Wambaugh, Joseph. *The Blooding*. New York: Perigord/William Morrow, 1989.

Early Articles about DNA

Altman, Lawrence K. "New DNA Test Offers Biological 'Fingerprints' for Crime Fight." *New York Times*, 4 February 1986.

Hilts, Philip J. "New Crime Identification Tool Devised; DNA Analysis May Be More Accurate Than Checking Fingerprints." *Washington Post*, 20 September 1987.

Articles

"Va. Man Held on Murder Count." *Washington Post*, 22 January 1988.

"Slaying Suspect Linked to Other Deaths." *Washington Post*, 18 March 1988.

"Va. Murder Suspect Indicted in Two Additional Slayings." *Washington Post*, 12 April 1988.

Priest, Dana. "Arlington Reopens 1984 Rape-Murder Case." *Washington Post*, 4 May 1988.

Williams, Paige. "For First Time, DNA Findings Ruled Admissible in Va. Court." *Washington Post*, 7 July 1988.

"Genetic Test Trial Opens in Arlington; Prosecutor Says New Evidence Is Vital to Rape-Murder Case." *Washington Post*, 12 July 1988.

"Defendant Said to Ask about Slaying." *Washington Post*, 13 July 1988.

Williams, Paige. "DNA Test Evidence Explained to Jury in Va. Slaying Case." *Washington Post*, 14 July 1988.

Hsu, Evelyn. "Defendant Denies He Is Killer; Va. Man Testifies in Genetic Trial." *Washington Post*, 15 July 1988.

———. "Va. Man Guilty in Trial Using DNA Evidence; Material Aided Murder Conviction." *Washington Post*, 16 July 1988.

———. "Jury Sentences Va. Man to Death for Rape-Murder" *Washington Post*, 17 July 1988.

"Arlington Convict Faces New Charge of Murder." *Washington Post*, 19 July 1988.

Bohn, John. "Fairfax Brings Charges Based on Genetic Evidence." *Washington Post*, 21 July 1988.

Green, Frank, and Ed Briggs. "Spencer Trial Begins in Davis Rape-Slaying." *Richmond Times-Dispatch*, 20 September 1988.

Green, Frank. "DNA Expert Testifies in Spencer Trial." *Richmond Times-Dispatch*, 21 September 1988.

―――. "Closing Arguments Are Expected Today in Spencer Case." *Richmond Times-Dispatch*, 22 September 1988.

―――. "Spencer Given Death Penalty." *Richmond Times-Dispatch*, 23 September 1988.

"Rapist-Murderer Gets 2nd Death Sentence in Va." *Washington Post*, 23 September 1988.

Priest, Dana. "Pardon Urged for Man Convicted in Va. Murder; New Evidence in 1984 Arlington Slaying Points to Richmond Felon." *Washington Post*, 12 October 1988.

―――. "Arlington Detective's Hunch Pays Off in Circumstantial Murder Case." *Washington Post*, 13 October 1988.

―――. "Rapist-Slayer in Virginia Given 2nd Death Sentence." *Washington Post*, 5 November 1988.

―――. "Va. Man Pardoned after Five Years in Prison; Baliles Acts after Evidence Links Murder to Arlington Killer." *Washington Post*, 5 January 1989.

Green, Frank. "Under Death Sentence Again, Spencer Blasts City, Witnesses." *Richmond Times-Dispatch*, 28 February 1989.

"Virginia Killer Is Sentenced to Death for the Third Time." *Washington Post*, 28 February 1989.

Williams, Joseph. "Prosecutors Say Data Link Slaying of Cho, 3 Others." *Richmond Times-Dispatch*, 9 May 1989.

―――. "Fluids Found at Slaying Scene Are Said to Match Spencer's." *Richmond Times-Dispatch*, 10 May 1989.

―――. "Decision Is Expected Today on Amplified DNA Printing." *Richmond Times-Dispatch*, 11 May 1989.

―――. "Spencer Verdict Expected Today." *Richmond Times-Dispatch*, 12 May 1989.

―――. "Chesterfield Jury Convicts Spencer of Cho Murder." *Richmond Times-Dispatch*, 13 May 1989.

"Virginia Jury Gives Rapist-Slayer 4th Death Sentence." *Washington Post*, 13 May 1989.

Priest, Dana. "Wrongly Jailed Man Endures Ordeal by Fear." *Washington Post*, 17 July 1989.

"Killer's Appeal Fails." *Washington Post*, 10 January 1990.

"'Southside Strangler' Loses Case." *Washington Post*, 10 June 1990.

"Judge Sets Execution Date for Virginia Murderer of 4." *Washington Post*, 8 March 1994.

"Appeal from Death Row." *Washington Post*, 24 April 1994.

"Stay of Execution Denied." *Washington Post*, 27 April 1994.

Green, Frank, and Mike Allen. "Execution to End Landmark Spencer Saga." *Richmond Times-Dispatch*, 27 April 1994.

Green, Frank, Mike Allen, and Bob Piazza. "Spencer, Killer of Four, Is Executed." *Richmond Times-Dispatch*, 27 April 1994.

Baker, Peter. "In Grim Distinction, Va. Killer Is 1st to Die Based on DNA Test." *Washington Post*, 28 April 1994.

———. "Victims' Families Forgo Invitation to Va. Execution." *Washington Post*, 2 May 1994

Legal Case

Spencer v. Murray. U.S. Court of Appeals for the Fourth Circuit. 16 September 1993.

About Elizabeth Haysom and Jens Soering

Book

Englade, Ken. *Beyond Reason: The True Story of a Shocking Double Murder, A Brilliant and Beautiful Virginia Socialite, and a Deadly Psychotic Obsession*. New York: St. Martin's, 1990.

Articles

Sherwood, Tom. "2 Former U.-Va. Students Quizzed in London about Slayings." *Washington Post*, 7 June 1986.

———. "London Court Hold 2 Questioned in Va. Deaths; Slain Couple's Daughter, Son of Diplomat Said to Be Suspects." *Washington Post*, 10 June 1986.

Specter, Michael. "2 in London Indicted in Va. Slayings." *Washington Post*, 14 June 1986.

"Va. Murder Suspects Plead in Britain." *Washington Post*, 11 October 1986.

"Murder Suspects Face Extradition." *Washington Post*, 28 March 1987.

"Va. Slaying Suspect Returns." *Washington Post*, 10 May 1987.

Baker, Donald P. "Pair Accused in Murders Shared Paths; Haysom Trial to Open in Parents' Slaying." *Washington Post*, 24 August 1987.

———. "Unexpected Guilty Plea by Daughter; Wealthy Va. Couple Was Slain in 1985." *Washington Post*, 25 August 1987.

"England Allows Extradition of Suspect in Va. Slayings." *Washington Post*, 12 December 1987.

"Va. Murder Suspect's Appeal Denied [by House of Lords]." *Washington Post*, 2 July 1988.

"Haysom Slaying Suspect Makes Appeal." *Washington Post*, 5 August 1988.

"British Approve Extradition for Suspect in Va. Slayings." *Washington Post*, 11 August 1988.

"Rights Court Rules against W. German's Extradition to Va." *Washington Post*, 8 July 1989.

"Britain Conditions Extradition on U.S. Avoiding Death Penalty." *Washington Post*, 2 August 1989.

"Extradition Allowed." *Washington Post*, 22 November 1989.

"Diplomat's Son Arrives in Va. for Trial in 1985 Slayings." *Washington Post*, 13 January 1990.

"W. German Pleads Not Guilty in Deaths of Virginia Couple." *Washington Post*, 2 June 1990.

Miller, Richard. "Arguments in Soering Case Begin." *The Daily Progress* [Charlottesville], 4 June 1990.

————. "Opening Remarks Presented in Soering Case." *The Daily Progress* [Charlottesville], 5 June 1990.

Davey, Monica. "Soering Defense: She Did It." *Roanoke Times & World-News*, 5 June 1990.

Miller, Richard. "Probe's Early Findings Focus of Soering Trial." *The Daily Progress* [Charlottesville], 6 June 1990.

Davey, Monica. "Tapes: Soering Went Alone." *Roanoke Times & World-News*, 7 June 1990.

Poole, David M. "Letters Alluded to Killing Haysoms." *Roanoke Times & World-News*, 7 June 1990.

Miller, Richard. "Soering Jury Hears Taped Interrogation." *The Daily Progress* [Charlottesville], 7 June 1990.

Davey, Monica. "Haysom Slayings Acted Out." *Roanoke Times & World-News*, 8 June 1990.

Miller, Richard. "Detective Recounts Confession." *The Daily Progress* [Charlottesville], 8 June 1990.

Davey, Monica. "Jury Sees Evidence." *Roanoke Times & World-News*, 9 June 1990.

Miller, Richard. "Soering Injuries Avowed." *The Daily Progress* [Charlottesville], 9 June 1990.

Lovegrove, Richard. "Jurors Told Admission of Guilt a Lie: Former U.-Va. Student Accused of Killings." *Washington Post*, 10 June 1990.

Miller, Richard. "Testimony of Ex-lover Key to Trial." *The Daily Progress* [Charlottesville], 10 June 1990.

Miller, Richard. "Soering Jurors Mull Evidence from Murder Site." *The Daily Progress* [Charlottesville], 12 June 1990.

Davey, Monica. "Soering Kept Tickets, Bills in Dorm Room." *Roanoke Times & World-News*, 13 June 1990.

Miller, Richard. "Receipts Said to Bolster Alibi in Slaying Case." *The Daily Progress* [Charlottesville], 13 June 1990.

Davey, Monica. "Haysom Recalls Alibi Plot." *Roanoke Times & World-News*, 14 June 1990.

Poole, David M. "Tarnished Star Witness Takes Stand." *Roanoke Times & World-News*, 14 June 1990.

Miller, Richard. "Testimony Puts Blame on Soering." *The Daily Progress* [Charlottesville], 14 June 1990.

"Diplomat's Son Called Killings 'Greatest Thing,' Girlfriend Says." *Washington Post*, 15 June 1900.

Davey, Monica. "Haysom Admits Many Lies." *Roanoke Times & World-News*, 15 June 1990.

Miller, Richard. "Haysom Recounts Web of Lies." *The Daily Progress* [Charlottesville], 15 June 1990.

"Va. Couple's Slaying Called 'Absolute Horror Experience.'" *Washington Post*, 16 June 1990.

Davey, Monica. "Jury Hears Second Soering Confession." *Roanoke Times & World-News*, 16 June 1990.

Miller, Richard. "Soering Admitted Stabbings in Taped Confession." *The Daily Progress* [Charlottesville], 16 June 1990.

Davey, Monica. "Soering Clues Hard to Pin Down." *Roanoke Times & World-News*, 17 June 1990.

Poole, David M., "Missing Ticket Raises Questions." *Roanoke Times & World-News*, 17 June 1990.

Miller, Richard. "Soering Defense to Begin." *The Daily Progress* [Charlottesville], 17 June 1990.

————. "Defense Relies on Lies, Love." *The Daily Progress* [Charlottesville], 18 June 1990.

"Soering Says Ex-Girlfriend Killed Parents." *Washington Post*, 19 June 1990.

Davey, Monica. "Soering: 'I Had to Protect Her.'" *Roanoke Times & World-News*, 19 June 1990.

Miller, Richard. "Soering: She Killed Them." *The Daily Progress* [Charlottesville], 19 June 1990.

"Soering Calls Role in Slaying 'Major Mistake' of His Life." *Washington Post*, 20 June 1990.

Davey, Monica. "Soering Answers All, Except Why He Took the Blame." *Roanoke Times & World-News*, 20 June 1990.

Poole, David M. "Defense Tactic Switched as Trial Came to America." *Roanoke Times & World-News*, 20 June 1990.

Miller, Richard. "Soering Voices Regrets." *The Daily Progress* [Charlottesville], 20 June 1990.

Reed, David. "Soering Found Guilty in Grisly Murders of Girlfriend's Parents." *Washington Post*, 22 June 1990.

Davey, Monica. "Jury Finds Soering Guilty." *Roanoke Times & World-News*, 22 June 1990.

————. "Jurors: Evidence Was Convincing, Soering Was Not." *Roanoke Times & World-News*, 22 June 1990.

Poole, David M. "Defense's Points Dulled with Ridicule." *Roanoke Times & World-News*, 22 June 1990.

Miller, Richard. "Jury: Soering Should Serve Two Life Terms." *The Daily Progress* [Charlottesville], 22 June 1990.

————. "Sock Print Moved Jurors to Convict Soering." *The Daily Progress* [Charlottesville], 24 June 1990.

Poole, David M. "Soering Trial Full of Culture Shocks." *Roanoke Times*, 24 June 1990.

"Soering Gets 2 Life Terms in Va. Killings." *Washington Post*, 5 September 1990.

Lillich, Richard B. "The Soering Case." *The American Journal of International Law* 85.1 (January 1991): 128-149.

"Va. Court Upholds Murder Convictions." *Washington Post*, 17 March 1992.

Zack, Ian. "Trial and Error." *The Daily Progress* [Charlottesville], 21 January 1996.

Baker, Donald P. "Diplomat's Son Back in Court; He Seeks to Overturn Conviction in Murdering of Girlfriend's Parents." *Washington Post*, 10 December 1996.

"New Trial Rejected." *Washington Post*, 23 April 1997.

Fain, Paul. "Murder Ink: Imprisoned for the Double Murder He Committed as a UVA Student, Jens Soering Now Aims for the Bestseller List." *Charlottesville News and Arts*, 8 December 2003.

Conley, Jay. "Haysom Murders, 20 Years Ago Today: Blood, Sweat and Convictions." *Roanoke Times*, 3 April 2005.

Sizemore, Bill. "No Hope for Jens Soering: Prisoner's Story Shows How to Survive." *Virginian-Pilot* [Norfolk], 18 February 2007.

Sluss, Michael, and Laurence Hammack. "Kaine Requests Jens Soering's Prison Transfer." *Roanoke Times*, 16 January 2010.

Sluss, Michael. "Lawmakers Opposed to Convicted Murderer Jens Soering's Transfer." *Roanoke Times*, 23 January 2010.

Bowman, Rex. "Justice Department: Soering Will Stay in Virginia." *Roanoke Times*, 8 July 2010.

———. "Jens Soering Still Hoping for Release." *Roanoke Times*, 29 July 2010.

———. "Notorious Murderer Jens Soering Denied Parole for Sixth Time." *Roanoke Times*, 19 August 2010.

Legal Case

Soering v. Deeds. U.S. Court of Appeals for the Fourth Circuit. 30 June 2000.

By Jens Soering, in Chronological Order

"On Penitence and Penitentiaries: A Prison Inmate Tells How Centering Prayer Brought Him to the Truth of Lent and Easter." *National Catholic Reporter*, 19 March 2004.

"Much Sadder Sentence." *America*, 29 March 2004.

"Another Easter Statistic: Is Jesus a Typical Culprit in the Never-Ending War on Crime?" *America*, 12 April 2004.

"The Perils of Freedom: Released Prisoners Face a Hostile World." *America*, 5 July 2004.

"Turning Tony into Tonya: Juveniles Raped in Adult Prisons Face 'Death Sentence' of HIV." *National Catholic Reporter*, 19 November 2004.

"The Bad Thief: A Kind of Prophet." *America*, 6 December 2004.

"The Carrot and the Sticks: Preventing Crime—What Works, What Doesn't, What the Future Holds." *America*, 21 March 2005.

"Uncorrected Failures of the Juvenile Justice System." *The Christian Century*, 18 September 2007.

"A Prisoner's Story: 37 Years behind Bars, One Year of Freedom." *America*, 21 April 2008.

"Life Without Parole: The Story of Liam Q." *The Christian Century*, 12 August 2008.

By Elizabeth Haysom

Glimpses from Inside. Columns. *The Fluvanna Review*, 2003-2008. www .fluvannareview.com.

See also Provence, Lisa. "Review Upheaval: Two Freelancers Quit over New Column." *The Hook* [Charlottesville], 3 April 2003.

About the Death of John Kowalczyk

Articles

"Hyman-Kowalczyk" (Wedding Announcement). *Washington Post*, 21 November 1979.

Murdoch, Joyce. "Slain Va. Builder Said He Feared for His Life." *Washington Post*, 13 June 1993.

Davis, Patricia, and Robert O'Harrow Jr. "Slain Developer Was Trying to Rebuild His Life; Va. Victim Was Struggling Back from Personal, Business Failure." *Washington Post*, 16 June 1993.

———. "Va. Police Believe Man Knew Killer; No Motive or Suspect in Builder's Slaying." *Washington Post*, 17 June 1993.

O'Harrow, Robert Jr. "Police Theorize on Killer's Escape." *Washington Post*, 18 June 1993.

Weil, Martin, and Robert O'Harrow Jr. "Lawyer Questioned in Slaying Apparently Attempts Suicide." *Washington Post*, 20 June 1993.

"Lawyer Recovering after Apparent Overdose." *Washington Post*, 21 June 1993.

Davis, Patricia, and Bill Miller. "Reston Lawyer Passed Polygraph, Attorney Says." *Washington Post*, 22 June 1993.

O'Harrow, Robert, Jr., and Bill Miller. "Police Identify Type of Handgun Used to Kill Fairfax Builder." *Washington Post*, 25 June 1993.

Davis, Patricia, and Bill Miller. "Investigation of Kowalczyk Killing Leads to a Maze; Police Suspect Several People Were Involved; Documents Detail Victim's Feuds with In-Laws." *Washington Post*, 26 June 1993.

O'Harrow, Robert, Jr., and Bill Miller. "Divorce Papers Depict Kowalczyk Under Siege; Builder Was Tailed by Private Detectives." *Washington Post*, 3 July 1993.

Miller, Bill, and Patricia Davis. "Police Suspect Hit Man in Virginia Slaying; Informer Claims He Was Offered Job of Killing Builder, Sources Say." *Washington Post*, 27 July 1993.

Miller, Bill. "Zumwalt Says Pressure Led to Pills; Lawyer Talks about Ties to Slain Builder." *Washington Post*, 31 July 1993.

Davis, Patricia, and Peter Baker. "Slain Builder's Former In-Laws Found Dead; Bodies Discovered in Fla. Apartment in Apparent Suicide-Slaying." *Washington Post*, 5 August 1993.

Davis, Patricia, and Bill Miller. "Note Asserts Innocence of Couple; Case of Slain Builder Turns to W.Va. Man." *Washington Post*, 6 August 1993.

O'Harrow, Robert, and Bill Miller. "Kowalczyk Case Lacks Evidence; Police Haven't Linked Builder's Former In-Laws to His Death." *Washington Post*, 7 August 1993.

Achenbach, Joel. "Till Death Do Us Part: John Kowalczyk Cheated in Work and Play and Love. This Made People Mad. It made One Person Very Mad. A Modern Whodunit." *Washington Post*, 5 September 1993.

Davis, Patricia, and Bill Miller. "Man Held in Kowalczyk Case: Prosecutor Says Ex-Wife's Father Paid for Killing." *Washington Post*, 21 September 1993.

Davis, Patricia, and Robert O'Harrow Jr. "Police Say $20,000 Was Paid for Va. Killing; Suspect Allegedly Called Victim's Ex-Father-in-Law after Slaying." *Washington Post*, 22 September 1993.

Davis, Patricia, and Bill Miller. "Disappearance Casts Resort Worker as Deadly Drama's Mystery Man." *Washington Post*, 30 September 1993.

———. "After a Year, Mystery Still Shrouds Builder's Death; Vienna Slaying Case Marked by Custody Battle, Suicide, Disappearance." *Washington Post*, 10 June 1994.

Davis, Patricia. "Body in W.Va. May Be Tied to '93 Case; Victim Possibly a Suspect in Fairfax Builder's Slaying." *Washington Post*, 14 June 1994.

Douglas, John. "Body Found in Well Is Figure in Va. Slaying; Remains Identified as James Alting, Sought in Contract Killing of Builder." *Washington Post*, 29 June 1994.

Miller, Bill. "Suicide Note Released: Man Denies Slaying Former Son-in-Law; Letter Implies 'Shady' Figures Shot Va. Builder." *Washington Post*, 7 July 1994.

Davis, Patricia. "Suspect in Fairfax Builder's Slaying Disputes Jailer's Testimony." *Washington Post*, 9 November 1994.

———. "Prosecutor Outlines Va. Slaying Case; Builder's Death Tied to 'Assassin's Bullet.'" *Washington Post*, 24 November 1994.

"Jury Selection Begins in Murder-for-Hire Trial." *Washington Post*, 29 November 1994.

Davis, Patricia. "Fairfax Jury Pool Picked in '93 Slaying of Builder; Trial to be Lengthy by County Standards." *Washington Post*, 1 December 1994.

———. "Prosecutor in Va. Murder-for-Hire Trial Says Defendant Told Co-Worker of Plan." *Washington Post*, 2 December 1994.

———. "Man Testifies Defendant Told Him of Murder Plot; Co-Worker Says He Was Asked to Aid in Killing." *Washington Post*, 3 December 1994.

———. "Phone Calls Cited in Murder-For-Hire Case; Defendant, Victim's Former In-Law Were in Touch, Prosecutor Says." *Washington Post*, 6 December 1994.

Tousignant, Marylou, and Patricia Davis. "Man Testifies His Father Never Threatened Slain Va. Builder." *Washington Post*, 7 December 1994.

Davis, Patricia, and Marylou Tousignant, "Woman Testifies That Murder Defendant Was in W.Va. at Time of Fairfax Shooting." *Washington Post*, 8 December 1994.

Davis, Patricia. "Murder Trial a Dramatic Sight Unseen; Lack of Spectators Is the Latest Twist in the Case of Slain Fairfax Builder." *Washington Post*, 8 December 1994.

Davis, Patricia, and Marylou Tousignant. "Private Eye Tells of Following Kowalczyk; Murder Trial Witness Says He Was Hired to Prove Va. Builder Was a 'Womanizer.'" *Washington Post*, 9 December 1994.

Davis, Patricia. "Fairfax Murder-for-Hire Case Goes to Jury; Prosecutor Says Shambaugh Implicated by Telephone Calls to Victim's Ex-Father-in-Law." *Washington Post*, 10 December 1994.

———. "Man Convicted of Conspiring to Kill Va. Builder." *Washington Post*, 14 December 1994.

Davis, Patricia, and Marylou Tousignant. "W.Va. Man Gets 18-Year Term in Builder's Slaying." *Washington Post*, 15 December 1994.

Davis, Patricia. "Specialists Say Shambaugh Could Face Retrial on Murder Count." *Washington Post*, 22 December 1994.

"Retrial Set in Slaying of Va. Builder." *Washington Post*, 26 January 1995.

Fountain, John W. "W.Va. Man Pleads Guilty in Fairfax Builder's Slaying; Groundskeeper Says He Was Accessory, Not Killer." *Washington Post*, 8 March 1995.

Legal Case

Shambaugh V. Johnson. United States District Court. 29 September 2008.

About Earl Washington Jr.

Books

Edds, Margaret. *An Expendable Man: The Near-Execution of Earl Washington Jr.* New York: New York University Press, 2003

Scheck, Barry, Peter Neufeld, and Jim Dwyer. *Actual Innocence: When Justice Goes Wrong and How to Make It Right.* Updated edition. New York: New American Library, 2003.

Articles

Masters, Brooke A. "Missteps on Road to Injustice; In Va., Innocent Man Was Nearly Executed." *Washington Post*, 1 December 2000.

Green, Frank. "Looking Forward to Starting Over." *Richmond Times-Dispatch*, 11 February 2001.

———. "Washington Released; Former Death Row Inmate Thanks Supporters on First Day Out." *Richmond Times-Dispatch*, 13 February 2001.

Glod, Maria. "False Confession Not Coerced, Judge Says; Retarded Man Was Nearly Executed." *Washington Post*, 24 June 2004.

Santos, Carlos. "Cleared Inmate Pursues Damages." *The Daily Progress* [Charlottesville], 24 April 2006.

Trice, Calvin R. "Lawyer: Investigator Broke Rules in Washington Case." *The Daily Progress* [Charlottesville], 25 April 2006.

———. "Attorney Testifies in Washington Case: False Confession Was Only Link to 1982 Murder." *The Daily Progress* [Charlottesville], 27 April 2006.

———. "Washington's Sister Testifies in Civil Suit." *The Daily Progress* [Charlottesville], 29 April 2006.

Green, Frank. "Former Inmate: Terrors of Death Row Still Haunt." *The Daily Progress* [Charlottesville], 3 May 2006.

———. "Washington Death-Row Lawsuit in Jury's Hands." *The Daily Progress* [Charlottesville], 5 May 2006.

———. "$2.25 Million Verdict in False Confession." *Richmond Times-Dispatch*, 6 May 2006.

———. "Case Centers on Agent with High Reputation." *Richmond Times-Dispatch*, 6 May 2006.

Markon, Jerry. "Wrongfully Jailed Man Wins Suit; Va. Officer Falsified Confession, Jury Rules." *Washington Post*, 6 May 2006.

Glod, Maria. "Former Death-Row Inmate Would Get $1.9 Million." *Washington Post*, 28 March 2007.

Scholarly Study

Leo, Richard A., and Richard J. Ofshe. "The Consequences of False Confessions: Deprivations of Liberty and Miscarriages of Justice in the Age of Psychological Interrogation." *The Journal of Criminal Law and Criminology* 88.2 (Winter 1998): 429-496.

Textbook

O'Hara, Charles E., and Gregory L. O'Hara. *Fundamentals of Criminal Investigation*. 6th edition. Springfield, IL: Charles C. Thomas, 1994.

About the Norfolk Four

Book

Wells, Tom, and Richard A. Leo. *The Wrong Guys: Murder, False Confessions, and the Norfolk Four*. New York: The New Press, 2008.

Articles

Jackman, Tom. "Three Men Seek Clemency in '97 Rape and Slaying in Norfolk." *Washington Post*, 10 November 2005.

"Justice in Norfolk?" Editorial. *Washington Post*, 5 January 2006.

Jackman, Tom. "Jurors Back Clemency for 'Norfolk 4.'" *Washington Post*, 6 January 2006.

"A Decision for Mr. Kaine." Editorial. *Washington Post*, 25 July 2006.

Jackman, Tom. "Conviction Overturned in 1997 Rape, Slaying." *Washington Post*, 1 December 2006.

"Make the Call." Editorial. *Washington Post*, 21 June 2007.

Jackman, Tom. "Conviction in 1997 Rape-Murder Is Affirmed; But 'Norfolk 4' Get Support from Ex-Attorneys General." *Washington Post*, 12 January 2008.

"Clear the Norfolk 4." Editorial. *Washington Post*, 13 January 2008.

Edds, Margaret. "The Norfolk Four: Clemency Petition Sits on Kaine's Desk." *The Hook* [Charlottesville], 10 April 2008.

Jackman, Tom. "Retired Agents Take Up Cause of 'Norfolk 4.'" *Washington Post*, 11 November 2008.

"Clemency for the Norfolk Four." Editorial. *Washington Post*, 11 November 2008.

Jackman, Tom. "Clemency Campaign Renews Misery; Parents of Slain Woman in Agony over Effort to Pardon the 'Norfolk 4.'" *Washington Post*, 15 December 2008.

———. "Grisham's Passion Project: A 'Norfolk 4' Screenplay." *Washington Post*, 8 July 2009.

Jackman, Tom, and Anita Kumar. "3 of 'Norfolk 4' Conditionally Pardoned in Rape, Killing." *Washington Post*, 7 August 2009.

"Kaine's Full Statement in 'Norfolk 4' Case." *Washington Post*, 7 August 2009.

"Statement of John and Carol Moore." *Washington Post*, 7 August 2009.

Toobin, Jeffrey. "The Wrong Guys." *The New Yorker*, 24 August 2009.

Legal Case

Tice v. Johnson. United States District Court. 14 September 2009.
Tice v. Johnson. United States District Court. 19 November 2009.

About Beverly Monroe

Book

Taylor, John. *The Count and the Confession: A True Mystery*. New York: Random House, 2002.

Articles

Blumenthal, Ralph. "A Virginia Tale of Love and Death, Suspicions and Doubt." *New York Times*, 22 February 2000.

Frey, Jennifer. "Death without an Ending: Ten Years after Her Lover Was Shot, Beverly Monroe Awaits a Final Verdict." *Washington Post*, 26 June 2002.

Kirsch, Laura. "Where's the Truth? False Confessions, Police Interrogations, and the Case of Beverly Anne Monroe." *The Forensic Examiner*, Fall 2006.

Legal Case

Monroe v. Angelone. United States District Court. 28 March 2002.

About the Shootings at Virginia Tech

Books

April 16: Virginia Tech Remembers. Ed. Roland Lazenby et al. New York: Plume, 2007.

Cullen, Dave. *Columbine*. New York: Twelve / Hachette, 2009.

Lebrun, Marcel. *Books, Blackboards, and Bullets: School Shootings and Violence in America.* Lanham, MD: Rowan & Littlefield, 2009.

Roy, Lucinda. *No Right to Remain Silent: The Tragedy at Virginia Tech.* New York: Harmony / Random, 2009.

Articles

Bechtel, Mark. "From the Beginning: Virginia Tech Football Has Not Always Been Powerful, But It Has Always Been Colorful." *Sports Illustrated,* 13 January 2000.

Cho, David [no relation], and Amy Gardner. "An Isolated Boy in a World of Strangers; Cho's Behavior Alarmed Some Who Knew Him." *Washington Post,* 21 April 2007.

Schulte, Brigid. "Killer's Parents Describe Attempts over the Years to Help Isolated Son." *Washington Post,* 31 August 2007.

Vargas, Theresa. "Va. Tech's Norris Hall to House Peace Center." *Washington Post,* 21 December 2007.

Somashekhar, Sandhya, and Sari Horwitz. "A Year after Massacre, Family Lives 'in Darkness': Parents of Va. Tech Gunman Secluded." *Washington Post,* 12 April 2008.

Official Report

Mass Shootings at Virginia Tech: Report of the Review Panel, August 2007. *Addendum,* November 2009.